ACKNOWLEDGEMENTS

I wish to thank the following people:

Kate Davey, for the illustrations.

Liz Archibald and Jennifer Peck, for proof reading.

Brighton Children's Library for helping me in some of my research for the book.

The Nina West Nurseries, in London, who tried out and provided some of the practical ideas.

All the friends who have helped to promote the Open-Sez-Me books.

OPEN-SEZ-ME

FOREWORD

Every child has a thirst for knowledge, a need that can be best satisfied through constructive play activities. However, this is not an easy task. Tapping the energy of the very young, whether in a home or nursery situation, places great demands on the ingenuity of the carer.

A common and useful approach is to relate activities with children to the time of year and to festivals occuring at that time. The problem is that to prepare an interesting and varied seasonal project can mean consulting one book for a story, another for an art idea, another for some background information and yet another for a recipe. Open-Sez-Me provides a comprehensive compendium of ideas for the carers of 2 to 7 year old children within one text. The provision of background material together with suggested activities of different types will, I hope, provide inspiration for a wide range of festival and nature-related projects.

I have worked with pre-school children for over twenty years, ten of which were spent running my own nursery. I found there was a distinct lack of available material for the non-Christian festivals which was suitable for this age group. In Open-Sez-Me, I have included festivals from a number of different cultures.

All in all, Open-Sez-Me is the book I would have loved to have had in my nursery. I do hope you have fun with the book and that it lightens the burden of those sticky moments when you say to yourself:

'WHAT SHALL WE DO WITH THE CHILDREN TODAY?'

CONTENTS

DECEMBER

FACTS   PAGE

December (Meaning of)	11
Christmas Past and Present	13
Christmas Day - Boxing Day	13
Carol Singing - Christmas Tree - Giving of Gifts	14
Mistletoe - Robins	14
St Nicholas - Santa Claus	15
Traditional Food	16
Christmas around the World - Austria - Belgium	16
Bulgaria - Brazil - Britain - Chile	17
Congo - Czechoslovakia - Denmark - France - Germany	18
Greece - Hungary	19
Italy - Norway - Mexico	20
Poland	21
Russia - Spain - Sweden	22
U.S.A	23
What is a Crystal?	27
Hanukkah	38
What Happens During Hanukkah Time	39
What is a Dreidel?	39
Kwanzaa	44
The Nguzo Saba - Kwanzaa Symbols	44

THINGS TO DO

Making a Christingle	19
Making a Pinata	21
Candle Head-Dress for St Lucia	23
Angels - Bells - Candles	24
Crackers - Christmas Cards	25
Christmas Tree 1 - Christmas Tree 2	26
Frosty Patterns with Paint and for the window	27
Lanterns - Snowstorm	28
Star, Bells and Snowflakes Mobile	29
Dreidel Game	39
A Dreidel Mobile - A Spinning Dreidel	40
A Menorah - Hanukkah Card	41
Kwanzaa Cards	45

COOKING

Yule Log — 30
Icing for the Yule Log — 31
Christmas Tree Cake — 31
Candle Cake — 31
Mince Pies — 32
Sponge Snowperson — 33
Christmas Biscuits — 34
Potato Latkes — 42
Apple Sauce — 42
Kuchlich (Butter Biscuits) — 43
Karamu Feast — 46
Groundnut Stew — 46
Couscous — 47

STORIES AND SONGS

Who Sleeps in December? — 12
Suggested Songs for Christmas — 36
The Story of Hanukkah — 38
Suggested Songs for Hanukkah — 43

POEMS

The Picman — 34
In The Week That Christmas Comes — 35
The North Wind Doth Blow — 35
Who Saw? — 36
Let's Be — 37

JANUARY

January (Meaning of)   48
New Year Past and Present   49
Brazil - Chile - China - Denmark - England   49
Germany - Greece - Holland - Hungary - Israel   50
India - Iran - Italy   50
Japan   51
Russia - Scotland   52
Spain - Vietnam   55
All About Worms   57
Chinese New Year   59
The Feast of Lanterns   62

THINGS TO DO

Janus Mask - Forcing Buds Indoors   56
Make A Wormery   58
A Chinese Lantern - A Dragon's Head - Masks   62
A Chinese Dragon - A Dragon Frieze   63

COOKING

Kuri Kinton   51
Black Bun   53
Petticoat Tails   54
Chinese Dumplings   64
Crispy Mo Fu   65
Chinese New Year Cake   65
New Year Cookies   66
Bean Sprouts   66

STORIES AND SONGS

Suggested Songs for January   56
New Year in Japan   52
Suggested Songs for Japanese New Year   52
The Legend of the Animals   60
Suggested Songs for Chinese New Year   61

POEMS

A Poem Which is Told by a Bird   58

FEBRUARY

February (Meaning of)   67
St Bride's Day   68
What do Birds Eat?   69
Tu B'Shvat   72
Candlemas Festival   76
Setsubun Festival   77
Carnival Around the World   78
America - Austria - Brazil - England   78
Germany - Italy - Mexico - Spain - Trinidad   79
Easter Pretzel   80
St Valentine's Day   85

THINGS TO DO

Making a Bird Cake   69
A Bird Table   69
Talking about Milk   70
Making Yoghurt   70
Making Butter   71
Counting and Touching Fruits Activity   72
Making a Palm Tree   73
Bark Rubbings and Wood Shavings   73
Growing Parsnip and Carrot Tops   74
Make Your Own Charcoal   74
Making Recycled Paper   75
Candle Pictures   76
Egg Experiment   76
Bean Activities   77
Making Masks   81
Musical Instruments   81
A Drum   82
Sandpaper Scratcher   82
Calabashes   82
Making a Valentine Card   86
Love Potions   87

COOKING

Making Yoghurt   70
Making Butter   71
Pretzels   80
Fish Balls   83
Pineapple Sherbet   83
Banana Bread   84
Valentine Tea Biscuits   88

FEBRUARY

STORIES AND SONGS

The Story of Bridget   68
Suggested Songs for February   71
My Setsubun   77
Suggested Songs for Setsubun   77
Three Bread Rolls   81
Suggested Songs for Carnival   84
Suggested Songs for Valentine's Day   86
Cupid and Psyche   89

POEMS

The Cow   71
Roses are Red   86

MARCH

Purim   90
Celebrating Purim   90
St David's Day   96
Daffodil Sunday   97
Hina-Matsuri   98
St Patrick's Day   100
The Shamrock   101

THINGS TO DO

Fun with Fruit Activity - A Scroll of Esther   91
Paper Plate Masks - A Gragger   91
Tambourines with Paper Plates   92
Make a Daffodil   96
Make a Hina-Matsuri Doll   98
How to Make an Origami Doll   99
Mixing Green for the Shamrock   101
Potato Print Snakes   101
Snake from a Plate - Sprouting a Potato   102
Shamrocks and Snakes from Baker's Clay   103

COOKING

Purim Biscuits   93
Poppy Seed Biscuits   94
Chick-Peas with Tomatoes   94

STORIES AND SONGS

The Story of Esther   90
Songs Sung at Purim   95
The Story of St David   97
Girls Day   99
Suggested Songs for Hina-Matsuri   99
Suggested Songs for St Patrick's Day   103

POEMS

The Daffodil   96

SUGGESTED BOOKS TO READ   104

DECEMBER

'Cold December brings the sleet,
Blazing fire and Christmas treat'

Its name comes from the Latin word **decem**, meaning ten. The Saxons called it Winter Monath, but after many of them became Christians, they renamed it **Heligh Monath** or Holy Month.

WHO SLEEPS IN DECEMBER?

A story to read

The year is nearly over, there's a stillness in the air. The ground is covered with snow, and children can be seen building snowpeople and tobogganing down the hilly slopes.

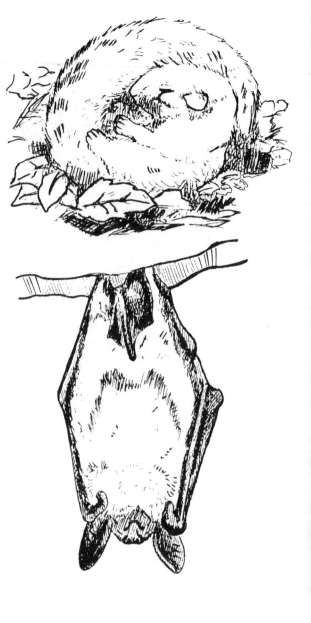

The birds can't be seen, because they have flown off to find the sun, or are keeping warm in sheltered places.

Families of rats and mice make warm nests in the hay. They come out only at night for food and to play.

When it is very cold, some animals go to sleep. This kind of sleep is called hibernation, and can last for months. It helps the animals to get through the winter when there isn't much food about. Their bodies become cold and they hardly breathe at all.

Hamsters go to sleep in winter, but may wake up every five days or so to feed on food which they have stored away.

Hedgehogs go to sleep in winter. Sometimes they sleep in piles of garden rubbish. Every two or three days they wake up to feed on lovely worms.

Bats hibernate in a cave or in roof tops. They hang upside-down and go to sleep.

Tortoises can bury themselves in the ground. They stay underground until the warm weather returns. So if you have a tortoise at home you should let it go to sleep by placing it in a box of hay in a cool place.

Frogs hibernate in the mud at the bottom of the pond. Snails hibernate under rocks.

When spring time comes, after a sleepy winter, look outside and you will see that all these animals have woken up.

CHRISTMAS PAST & PRESENT

In the following section you will find a wealth of information relating to customs and activities for the December festivals of Christmas and St Nicholas. I hope you will find it useful to draw on this information in a way that suits your needs. In my school, we did a successful collage of 'Christmas Throughout the World'.

CHRISTMAS DAY - December 25th

This day is now observed throughout the Western world as the birthday of Christ.

Originally, pagan festivals were celebrated at the end of December. One of the earlier celebrations was the **Norse Yule** which symbolized the sun's rebirth after the winter solstice.

At that time people would go out into the woods to cut Yule logs for their fires. They decorated their homes with holly and they collected mistletoe from the oak trees, to hang over their doorways thus keeping away evil spirits.

It was only during the Middle Ages that the two festivals merged and the Yule logs and Yule candles became a traditional part of Christmas. These symbolized fire and light, so too did the custom of the candlelit Christmas tree, which was believed to shelter the woodland spirits when other trees lost their leaves.

BOXING DAY - December 26th

According to the Church Calender, the day after Christmas is St Stephen's Day. It is more commonly known as Boxing Day, because of the custom of giving **boxes** or presents of money to servants, tradesmen, and those in public service. In England it is also a Bank Holiday.

CAROL SINGING

The custom of singing Christmas carols is very old, The earliest English collection was published as long ago as 1521.

CHRISTMAS TREE

The Christmas tree first appeared in Germany in the 18th century. It became popular in England after Queen Victoria's husband, the Prince Consort (who was German by birth), had provided one for a children's party at Windsor Castle in 1841. Today, in Trafalgar Square in London you will find the most famous tree, which has become an annual gift from the people of Oslo.

GIVING GIFTS

This recalls the gifts brought to the Infant Jesus by the Three Wise Men as told in the Bible.

MISTLETOE

This is a sacred pagan plant and a traditional Christmas symbol. Like holly and other evergreens it was believed that they provided refuge for woodland spirits until other trees regained their leaves.

The mistletoe was believed to hold the life of the oak tree when the tree appeared to be dead in winter. According to the Druids, the pearly berries were regarded as the seminal fluid of the oak and therefore of the oak tree god or spirit. For this reason, it was held to be a charm to induce fertility, and the present-day custom of kissing under a sprig of mistletoe probably derives from this.

ROBINS

The robin's red breast has given rise to many legends through the centuries. One says that the robin was singed while taking water to sinners burning in hell. Another says that it wounded itself while trying to lessen the agony of Christ's crown of thorns, and was splashed with a drop of his blood.

ST NICHOLAS - December 6th

This is the festival of St Nicholas - but in Britain nowadays we celebrate him on Christmas Day as Santa Claus, or Father Christmas. Children elsewhere in Europe celebrate Saint Nicholas Day earlier in December. The children leave a shoe in the hearth to receive the presents he brings, and they leave a carrot for his horse.

The real St Nicholas was a bishop in Asia Minor, who died about A.D 342. He became the patron saint of Russia and of children, sailors, merchants, and those in sudden danger.

He is often shown in pictures standing next to three children in a tub. The story is told of how the three girls had been killed and pickled in a famine and given to Nicholas for food. But he brought them back to life. He is said to have given three bags of gold as dowries to the three girls. (These bags of gold are the origin of the three gold balls, which is the sign hanging above a pawnbroker's shop). According to legend, St Nicholas left the money while the girls were asleep, and so began the custom of giving presents in secret on his feast day.

SANTA CLAUS

Santa Claus has a very special place in the hearts of most children. His present image is due to the work of a 19th century American poet, Clement Moore, who in his poem 'A Visit From St Nicholas', describes Father Christmas as chubby and plump, with cheeks like roses and a nose like a cherry, arriving on a reindeer-drawn sleigh.

The name Santa Claus originated from the Dutch for St Nicholas. Early Dutch settlers in America took this tradition with them. English settlers adopted it, and the shoe became a stocking and Santa Claus became the familiar white-haired, red-cloaked figure, who rides from the North Pole in a sledge drawn by reindeer, and enters the house by way of the chimney.

TRADITIONAL FOOD

Traditional food at Christmas time includes the flaming Christmas Pudding which was introduced in about 1670. A piece of holly is put on top and this is then set alight with whisky. This ritual comes from the ancient Celtic sun-worshipping festival. The flaming pudding tells the guest that winter will end and the sun will return.

The turkey is an American tradition, which became popular in England at the beginning of the 20th century. Before this, the traditional Christmas meat was a boar's head, beef or goose.

CHRISTMAS AROUND THE WORLD

In Austria the Christmas festival lasts two days. On Christmas Eve the family gather together for a meal of carp, since meat is not eaten at this time. Everyone attends Midnight Mass. On Christmas Day the special foods are roast goose, ham and fruitcake. The children receive their gifts on December 6th from St Nicholas, who scolds them if they have been naughty, and leaves presents of nuts, fruit, and sweets for those who have been good.

In Belgium, St Nicholas is portrayed as a tall thin man with long white hair, dressed in the robes of a bishop and wearing a high pointed hat. In his hand he holds a golden staff. His helper is called **Nicodemus**, who follows him, leading a donkey loaded with two large wicker baskets, called **panniers**, filled with toys and sweets. On the Eve of St Nicholas, the children place their shoes at the bottom of the chimney, and in each one they put a turnip or carrot for St Nicholas' donkey, then they sing:

"Saint Nicholas, friend of little school children,
Bring me some sweets for my two shoes.
I will always be good like a little lamb,
And I promise to say my prayers, in return for candy.
Come, come, Saint Nicholas, Tra-la-la".

The morning after, the vegetables have been replaced by toys and sweets.

In Bulgaria, farmers strike a blazing log in the fireplace, and then with each blow they make a wish for good health to the stock and land, and a bountiful harvest. The ashes are then gathered, money is hidden in them and placed in a tree to ensure a good crop.

In Brazil, Christmas comes in midsummer and the celebrations are held in the open air. The original Portuguese-Catholic customs have been modified by African, Indian and other influences, so Christmas celebrations and customs take many forms. There is the festival of the Three Kings and dance festivals such as the Fandango and the Cheganca. These are sometimes accompanied by the lighting of bonfires and firework displays. Families attend church at midnight on Christmas Eve and return home to a dinner of roast pig. The bringer of presents is Santa Claus (known as Papai Noel), who still comes dressed in his red suit.

In Britain, Christmas first began to assume its present significance as a holiday as well as a religious festival during the Middle Ages. In 1644 the keeping of Christmas was condemned by Puritans and was forbidden in England by an Act of Parliament.

Today it is a festive occasion celebrated by the giving of gifts, visiting friends and the eating of turkey and Christmas pudding.

In Chile, Christmas comes in the summer time. Nativity scenes and Christmas trees fill some homes. A Midnight Mass is held on Christmas Eve. The Christmas meal will include any kind of salad, special creamy cakes and chocolate biscuits. There are fairs and fiestas in many parts with big displays of national crafts such as handmade rugs, blankets and jewellery.

In the Congo, the African Christians sing carols wherever the Nativity story has become known, and go to church where gifts are given and received.

In Czechoslovakia, Christmas begins on December 5th, when the children receive presents of apples, nuts and sweets. At this time young boys go round the village with **wooden snakes**, cut out of wood. They go from house to house singing carols while one of the boys waves the snake and in return they receive a gift. A holiday fast, observed by many families, is broken when the first star appears on Christmas Eve, known as **Starry evening**. Families sit down to a traditional supper, this will include soup, fish (usually carp) with potato salad, special shaped bread and holiday cake with almonds and raisins.

In Denmark, Santa Claus is helped by small elves called the **Julenisse**. They carry a lantern to work by, and if children don't leave them something to eat, they can get quite hungry and grumpy. Traditionally home-made hearts are used to decorate the trees.

In Eastern France St Nicholas Day is on December 6th. This is the time when children receive sweets and gifts. When the children are asleep, little toys, sweets, and fruit are hung on the tree. Father Christmas leaves presents in their shoes which they have left by the fireplace. At midnight on Christmas Eve, people go to church where three masses are held. Afterwards the family tucks into a supper known as **reveillon**. This may consist of baked ham, roast fowl, salads, cake, fruit, bonbons, and wine.

In Germany the children receive their presents from a man dressed in white robes, wearing a golden crown and wings. The custom of giving a **Christingle** was started in the 18th century and still survives today.

MAKING A CHRISTINGLE

This is an orange, decorated to represent various aspects of the Christian belief.

YOU WILL NEED

An **orange** which represents the world, a **candle** which stands for the Light of the World, **sweets, nuts** and **raisins** symbolizing the animals and fruit of the earth, **red crêpe paper** which represents the blood of Christ and **cocktail sticks.**

METHOD

1. Slice the bottom of the orange, so that it will stand firm, fix a candle in its holder into the top and decorate the base with red crêpe paper.

2. Put the sweets, nuts and raisins onto one end of a cocktail stick and secure the other end into the orange.

In Greece, the festivities are celebrated in church and with the giving of presents. Roast pig will form the main part of the Christmas dinner, and their special greeting is **Eti Pola** which means **A Long Life to You**.

In Hungary as in many other countries in Europe, December 6th is the gift day for the children. When the first star appears on Christmas Eve, the Christmas feast begins. This consists of cabbage soup, horseshoe-shaped cakes filled with walnuts and poppy seeds, special bread twisted into decorative shapes, and small dumplings covered with poppy seeds and sugar.

In Italy the festivities last three weeks, from the beginning of the **Novena** (eight days preceding Christmas) until after the Twelfth Night. During the Novena, children go around reciting Christmas selections, and are given money. In some homes you might find a **presepio**, which is a miniature representation of the Holy Family and the manger. A rigid fast is observed during the 24 hours prior to Christmas Eve, and is followed by supper. After this, presents are drawn from the **Urn of Fate**.

On January 6th (Epiphany), the children are visited by **Befana**, a beautiful, smiling witch who climbs down chimneys to put presents in the shoes of good children. The not-so-good are supposed to get charcoal. Befana was a house-proud woman who entertained the three kings on their way to visit Jesus. For this reason, her gifts are distributed at Epiphany, the day which celebrates the visit of the three kings.

In Norway, seven kinds of **thaw** biscuit are baked to eat over the festival season. Norwegian tradition claims that the heat of all the ovens baking biscuits helps the winter snow to thaw!

In Mexico a Pinata party may be held at Christmas time. Pinata parties are also held in Mexico and Venezuela on the birthday of someone who has the same name as one of the saints.

A Pinata is a cheap pottery cooking jar, filled with toys and sweets. It can also be made out of papier mâché which is shaped into a ball or an animal, filled with sweets and toys, then hung from a doorway. The birthday child stands blindfolded under the Pinata. They are given a large stick and turned round and round. Then they have to try and hit the Pinata. Their friends shout directions and finally after several attempts the Pinata breaks and a cascade of toys and sweets is released and everyone scrambles to get a share.

MAKING A PINATA

This must be made at least a week in advance, to allow for plenty of time to dry. However if you haven't got time to make a Pinata from a balloon, use a strong brown paper bag and decorate it.

<u>YOU WILL NEED</u>

Round balloon, newspaper, 1/2 cup of flour mixed with water, crêpe paper cut into streamers, paint, string, scissors, small sweets and toys.

<u>METHOD</u>

1. Blow up the balloon. Tear the newspaper into 8cm (3") strips, paste the strips onto the balloon making sure there are several layers.

2. When the balloon is completely dry, cut a hole at the top and paint the balloon.

3. When the paint has dried, glue on paper streamers and fill the Pinata with sweets, nuts, and tiny toys. Hang it up with string.

In Poland the holiday fasting ends with the first star on Christmas Eve. The head of the household breaks an **oplatek**, a large, thin, consecrated wafer with each person and exchanges wishes for their health and happiness. These wafers are baked in cast-iron moulds and stamped with pictures of the nativity and blessed by the priest. In rural areas wafers are divided among cattle, horse and sheep.

The Christmas Eve supper, the **Wilia**, sometimes includes an extra place at the table for any stranger who might come knocking at the door. Traditionally a thirteen-course meal in memory of Christ and the twelve apostles would be prepared. The Christmas tree is decorated with coloured candles and decorated eggs. King Wenceslas is also remembered at this time. He was the King of Czechoslovakia, and so legend has it, a compassionate man. The carol, **Good King Wenceslas**, recalls one of his generous deeds when he helped a peasant.

In Russia, it is **Baboushka** who offered food and shelter to the three kings on their journey to Bethlehem, and it is she who delivers presents to children. Like Befana she did not accompany the kings because she felt she should tidy her house. When Baboushka finally reached Bethlehem, Jesus had left! She is supposed to be still seeking him and at Christmas when she sees a sleeping child and hears of good deeds, she leaves a toy from her basket then carries on with her journey.

In Spain, Christmas or **Nochebuena** is the time for fairs in many parts of Spain where toys, marzipan flowers, fruit, all kinds of food and figures for nativity scenes can be bought. Midnight Mass is held so Christmas dinner is eaten very late in the evening. A typical dinner may consist of turkey, roast suckling pig, or roast lamb, followed by all kinds of sweetmeats such as **Turron**, a kind of nougat, crystallized fruits and toasted almonds.

The children traditionally get their presents from the Three Wise Men as they travel through Spain on their way to Bethlehem. On the night before Epiphany, January 6th, children stuff hay or grain in their shoes and leave them on the balcony for the Wise Men's camels. In the morning the food is always gone, and sweets and toys are left in its place.

In Sweden, Finland and Norway, the Christmas season lasts a month from December 13th, St Lucia's day, until January 13th, St Knut's day. On December 13th, the oldest daughter in the household acts the part of St Lucia, Queen of Light. Dressed in white and wearing a crown of pine twigs decorated with candles, she wakes the rest of the family with a tray of coffee and newly baked Lucia buns. Schools will often hold a candle procession. Special foods are prepared, these include the **lutefisk**, dried cod which has to be soaked for 14 days. It is then boiled and can be served with a white sauce and potatoes.

On Christmas Eve the family gathers round a big kettle or iron pot for the ceremony of **dipping the kettle**. The **Dip** is a thick broth made from sausages, pork and corned beef. Everyone dips a piece of bread into the pot and eats. This is followed by lunch, which is usually an array of smörgasbord, and finishing with rice pudding. After this comes the lighting of the candles on the Christmas tree, carols, presents and a visit from Santa Claus known as **Jultomtem**.

CANDLE HEAD-DRESS For St Lucia

<u>YOU WILL NEED</u>

A4 paper, paint, glitter.

<u>METHOD</u>

1. Fold a piece of A4 paper in half longways then cut it along the crease. Glue these two pieces together to form a long strip.

2. Along this strip draw a line 4 cm (2") from the edge. Above this draw candles and then cut them out, leaving the band at the bottom. Decorate, then glue the ends together to form a head band.

In the U.S.A. Christmas is a collage of customs brought by its people from all over the world. Traditionally Christmas Eve was a time for reflective prayers and hymn singing. This was later replaced by a seven-day festival of dancing, feasting and singing.

THINGS TO DO

ANGELS

<u>YOU WILL NEED</u>

Empty toilet roll, paper, glitter, paint, glue.

<u>METHOD</u>

1. Cut out an angel shape in paper. Paint the toilet roll and the angel shape. When these have dried, apply glue and sprinkle glitter.

2. Glue the angel onto to the toilet roll, this can either be hung up or left free standing.

BELLS

These can be made by cutting out bell shapes and decorating with glitter, or by cutting the sections from an egg box and painting them yellow. Cut out holly leaves, paint them green and place at the top of the bell. Hang the bells from a coat hanger with cotton.

CANDLES

<u>YOU WILL NEED</u>

Empty toilet roll, thin card, paint, glitter, sticky shapes, glue, paper plate.

<u>METHOD</u>

1. Cut out candle flame shapes in card, paint yellow or red. Paint the paper plate.

2. Make a slit either side of the toilet roll and paint it. When the candle flame is dry, place in the slits.

3. Make a hole in the middle of the paper plate and secure the candle in it.

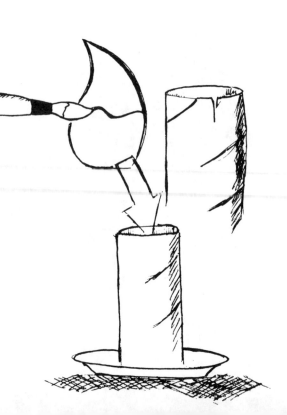

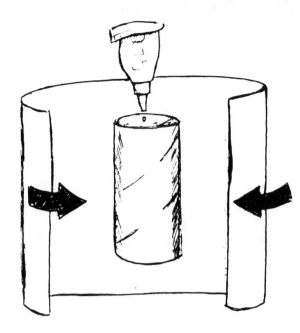

CRACKERS

YOU WILL NEED

Empty kitchen roll, white paper, ribbon or cotton, glue, sticky shapes and glitter, sweets or little presents.

METHOD

1. Cut enough paper to wrap round the kitchen roll and allow at least 8 cm (3") either end.

2. Glue shapes and glitter onto the paper. When dry wrap this around the kitchen roll.

3. Twist one end of the cracker first, then place the sweets or little presents inside. Then twist the other end carefully and secure each end with the ribbon or cotton.

CHRISTMAS CARDS

Fold some card in half and cut out one of the designs below. Decorate with paint, sticky shapes, glitter and cotton wool.

A FEW SUGGESTED DESIGNS FOR CHRISTMAS CARDS

BELLS   TREES   SNOWPEOPLE

CHRISTMAS TREE 1

<u>YOU WILL NEED</u>

10 toilet rolls, card, glue, green paint, string, cotton wool.

<u>METHOD</u>

Staple four rolls side by side, then three, then two. Staple the three onto the four and then the two onto the three and staple the last one on top and paint green. When dry, glue pinches of cotton wool on the tree. Thread the last one with string and hang up.

CHRISTMAS TREE 2

<u>YOU WILL NEED</u>

Two 15 cm (6") square cards, paint, cotton wool, toilet roll.

<u>METHOD</u>

1. Cut out the tree from both cards, fold both cards in half and paint green. When dry, decorate with coloured shapes and cotton wool.

2. Cut 5 cm (2") from the kitchen roll and cut four slits in it as shown. Paint red.

3. When dry, place the trees into the slits.

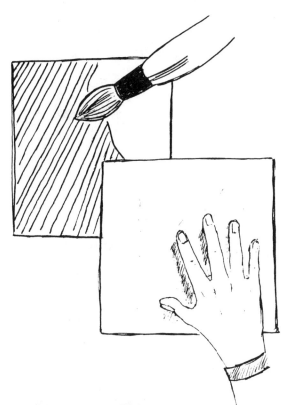

FROSTY PATTERNS with paint

YOU WILL NEED

White poster paint, thin paste, sheet of dark coloured card.

METHOD

Mix a little paste with the white paint and stir well. Brush the mixture thickly all over the card. Make patterns with your fingers in the white paste.

FROSTY PATTERNS for the window

YOU WILL NEED

Mixing bowl, sponge, cup and spoon, washing soda or Epsom salts, hot water from the tap, cotton wool.

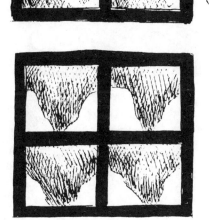

METHOD

1. Put a cup of washing soda and a cup of hot water into a bowl. Stir until the soda dissolves. With your sponge wipe the window with the liquid.

2. Leave it for 20 minutes, the water will disappear. This leaves the crystals, looking like frost. Glue small pieces of cotton wool at the bottom of the window to create a snow effect.

Try making different coloured frost by colouring your water with food colouring. Why not try blue to create a really frosty look. You can make frosty patterns in the summer time too!

WHAT IS A CRYSTAL?

Crystals are solid substances with a regular shape. Lots of things are crystals, for example sand, sugar, salt and glass. To find out which crystals dissolve pour on hot water. To change back into a crystal, leave in a warm place, until all the water dries up.

LANTERNS

YOU WILL NEED

Glue, sheet of A4 paper, scissors, glitter, paint, strip of paper 2 cm x 25 cm (1" x 10") for the handle.

METHOD

1. Fold the paper in half lengthwise and draw lines 2 cm (1") apart and 8 cm (3") long. Let the children cut along the lines.

2. Paint the lantern and handle. When dry, glue and glitter.

3. Attach the handle to the top of the lantern.

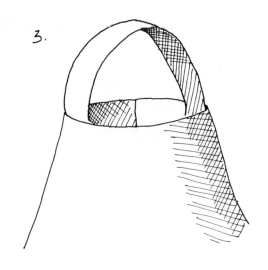

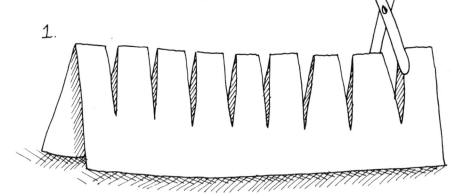

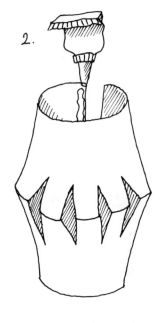

SNOWSTORM

YOU WILL NEED

A jar, water, desiccated coconut.

METHOD

Fill the jar with water and put some desiccated coconut into it. Create your snow storm by shaking the jar.

STARS, BELLS AND SNOWFLAKES MOBILE

YOU WILL NEED

Thin card, paper, glitter, glue, fluorescent paint, cotton.

METHOD

1. Cut out star and bell shapes then paint and decorate them.

2. Cut out some snow flakes by folding a piece of paper into a triangular shape, cut away little sections, then decorate.

3. Hang each one with a cotton thread from a coat hanger or a length of dowel.

Snowflakes can also be made from paper doilies by cutting each doily into different sized circles. These can be glued onto different lengths of thick cotton.

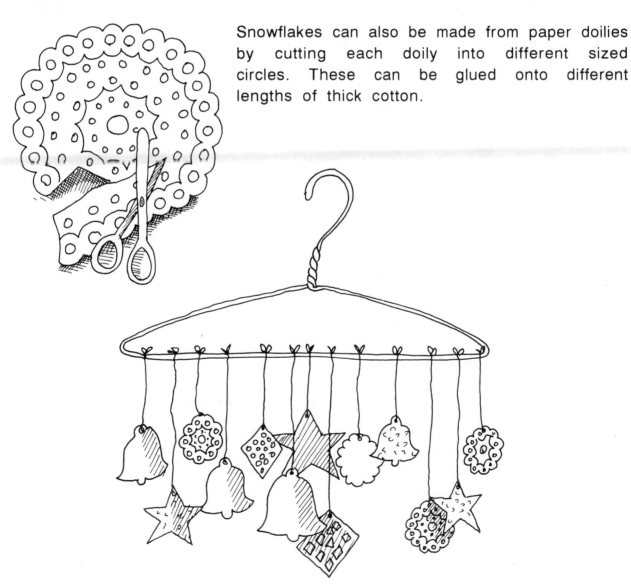

COOKING

YULE LOG

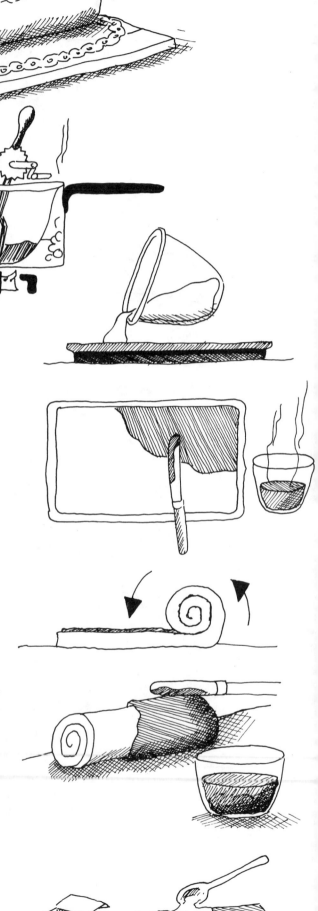

<u>YOU WILL NEED</u>

110 g (4 oz) caster sugar
110 g (4 oz) plain flour
3 eggs
1 tablespoon hot water
warmed jam

Oven temperature: 180 'C/350 'F/Gas 4

<u>METHOD</u>

1. Line a Swiss roll tin, 23 cm x 30 cm (9" x 12") with greaseproof paper.

2. Put the eggs and sugar in a large bowl, stand it over a pan of hot water and whisk until light and creamy - the mixture should be stiff enough to retain the impression of the whisk for a few seconds.

3. Sift half the flour over the mixture and fold in very lightly, using a tablespoon. Add the remaining flour in the same way and lightly stir in the hot water. Pour the mixture into the tin and bake near the top of the oven for 7-9 minutes, until golden-brown, well risen and firm.

4. Turn the cake onto some greaseproof paper. To make the sponge pliable, you can place the paper over a tea towel lightly wrung out in hot water. Trim the edges and spread the surface with warmed jam. Roll up with the aid of the paper, making the first turn firm, then roll lightly. Ice the log with Yule Log Icing (see next page). Alternatively you can coat the sponge with white sugar for a snowy effect.

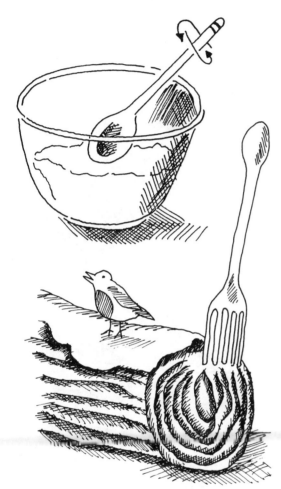

YULE LOG ICING

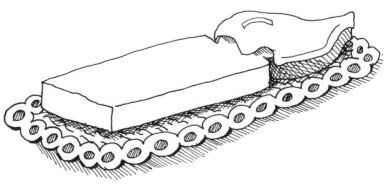

YOU WILL NEED

75 g (3 oz) butter
150 g (6 oz) icing sugar
1-2 tablespoons warm water
1 level tablespoon drinking chocolate, dissolved in a little water

METHOD

Cream the butter until soft and gradually beat in the sugar. Add the drinking chocolate. Coat the sponge with the mixture and make lines with a fork to represent the bark of a tree. Sprinkle with icing sugar for snow, and add a sprig of artificial holly or a model robin.

CHRISTMAS TREE CAKE

Follow the recipe for the Yule Log to step 3 then trim the cake into a Christmas tree. Use green colouring in the icing and decorate your tree with small jelly sweets.

CANDLE CAKE

Follow the recipe for the Yule Log to step 3 then trim the cake into the shape of a candle with a flame. Use yellow colouring in the icing sugar for a candle effect.

MINCE PIES

It is said that if you eat a mince pie on each of the twelve days of Christmas this will bring twelve happy months in the following year.

YOU WILL NEED

225 g (8 oz) plain flour
110 g (4 oz) margarine
1/4 teaspoon salt
4-5 tablespoons water, to mix
225 g (8 oz) mincemeat
1 egg, beaten, to glaze
Sieved icing sugar

Oven temperature: 170 'C/325 'F/Gas 3

METHOD

1. Sift the flour and salt into a bowl. Cut the margarine into the flour and rub in with the fingertips.

2. Sprinkle on the water and knead until smooth. Leave to rest in the fridge, wrapped in greaseproof paper and a polythene bag, for 30 minutes.

3. Knead again, roll out, cut into circles and place in greased tartlet tray. Save some pastry for lids.

4. Spoon the mincemeat into the pastry cases. (Brandy if desired, can be added to the mincemeat). Roll out the remaining pastry and cut to make lids. Place them on the cases and brush with the beaten egg.

5. Bake the pies in the centre of the oven for 20-25 minutes. Remove from the tins, cool and sprinkle with icing sugar.

SPONGE SNOWPERSON

YOU WILL NEED

110 g (4 oz) margarine
110 g (4 oz) self-raising flour
110 g (4 oz) sugar
vanilla essence
2 eggs, beaten
icing sugar, hot water
liquorice assortments

Oven temperature: 180 'C/350 'F/Gas 4

METHOD

1. Grease two 18 cm (7") sandwich tins and line the bases with a round of greased greaseproof paper.

2. Cream the margarine and sugar together until pale and fluffy. Add the egg, and a few drops of vanilla essence a little at a time.

3. Fold in half the flour, using a tablespoon, then fold in the rest.

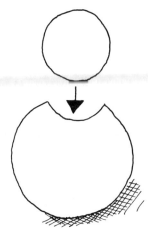

4. Pour the mixture into the tins and bake just above the centre of the oven for about 30 minutes. Cool on a rack.

5. Trim one of the cakes down to 12 cm (5") to form the head. Then remove a small semi-circle from the top of the larger cake so that the head can fit into the body.

6. Make some icing by mixing hot water with icing sugar. Join the two cake pieces by icing them together. Use the liquorice assortments for the snowperson's face, and for buttons down their front.

CHRISTMAS BISCUITS

YOU WILL NEED

225 g (8 oz) plain flour
110 g (4 oz) margarine
110 g (4 oz) castor sugar
a few drops of vanilla essence
small silver balls or jelly sweets

Oven temperature: 180 'C/350 'F/Gas 4

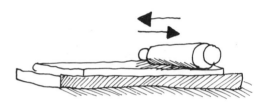

METHOD

1. Grease two baking trays.

2. Cream the margarine and sugar until fluffy. Add the essence a little at a time, beating after each addition.

3. Stir in the flour and mix to a fairly firm dough. Knead lightly and roll out to biscuit thickness on a floured board.

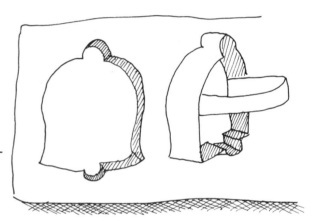

4. Cut into shapes using Christmas cutter shapes, and bake in the centre of the oven for 15-20 minutes, until firm and lightly browned.

5. Cool on a rack then decorate with icing sugar and small silver balls or little pieces of jelly sweets.

POEMS

THE PIEMAN

As I was going down Mincing Lane,
Mincing Lane on a Christmas Day,
'**Hot mince pies!**' a pieman cries,
'**Two for a penny, and look at the size!**'

Anon

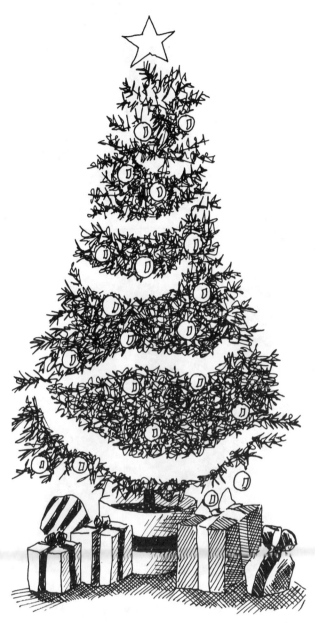

IN THE WEEK WHEN CHRISTMAS COMES

This is the week when Christmas comes.

Let every pudding burst with plums,
And every tree bear dolls and drums,
In the week when Christmas comes.

Let every hall have boughs of green
With berries glowing in between,
In the week when Christmas comes.

Let every doorstep have a song
Sounding the dark street along,
In the week when Christmas comes.

Let every steeple ring a bell
With a joyful tale to tell,
In the week when Christmas comes.

Let every night put forth a star
To show us where the heavens are.
In the week when Christmas comes.

Let every stable have a lamb
Sleeping warm beside its dam,
In the week when Christmas comes.

by Eleanor Farjeon

THE NORTH WIND DOTH BLOW

The North Wind doth blow
And we shall have snow,
And what will poor robin do then?
Poor thing!
He'll sit in a barn,
And keep himself warm,
And hide his head under his wing.
Poor thing!

Anon

WHO SAW?

It's Christmas time,
And the clock will chime 1 2 3 4.

Who saw the flames flickering in the night,
Dancing whirling in the light?

Who saw the wind that blows, it twists and turns,
As our fire slowly burns?

Who saw the robin pecking at the scarecrow's hat,
Being chased away by a big black cat?

Who saw the owl, calling to the moon,
And heard the sleigh-bell's merry tune?

Who saw the church mouse shiver in the cold,
And the Christmas fairy with wings of gold?

Who saw Mum and Dad creep slowly up the stairs,
And sleeping children free from cares?

The world will soon awake and we will say,

'It's here at last, it's Christmas day'

by Shirley West

Suggested Songs: **Santa Claus, White Bells**, from **Infant Joy, A Complete Repertoire of Songs**, published by University of London Press Ltd.

Carol, Under Bethl'em's Stars so Bright, Child for the World, Girls and Boys, Leave Your Toys, from **Festivals (All the Year)**, by Jean Gilbert, published by Oxford University Press.

Christmas is Joyful, Snowdrop Bells, from **Harlequin**, published by A & C Black.

Baboushka, Christmas Present, from **Singalive 12 Songs and a Cakewell**, by Donald Swann and Arthur Scholey, published by Collins.

The children can make costumes representing the different characters.

LET'S BE

Let's be snowflakes,
Whirling to the ground.
We make a soft white carpet,
Without a single sound.

Let's be fir trees,
Stretching to the sky.
See our branches swaying,
As the north wind hurries by.

Let's be Jack Frost,
Busy with his brush.
He leaves a silver lining,
On every tree and bush.

Let's be snowpeople,
With hats and scarves so gay.
When Mr Sun looks down on us,
We quickly run away.

Let's be Santa,
With his sack of toys.
Filling stockings to the brim,
For all the girls and boys.

Let's be reindeer,
Pulling Santa's sleigh.
With merry bells a-jingle,
We gallop on our way.

Anon

This Little Light of Mine, Amen, Shalom, Hevenu Shalom, from **Alleluya 77 Songs for Thinking People**, published by A & C Black.

Winds Through the Olive Trees, Junkanoo, Happy Christmas, Noel, Noel, Christmas Cake, When the Red, Red, Robin, from **Flying A Round**, published by A & C Black.

HANUKKAH

Hanukkah, the Jewish Feast of lights, begins on the evening of the 25th day of the Hebrew month called Kislev. This usually corresponds to the month of December. This festive occasion lasts for eight days, and each one is filled with songs, games, food, and the lighting of the Hanukkah candles.

Hanukkah reminds people of the miracle which took place in Israel over 2,000 years ago.

THE STORY OF HANUKKAH

A story to read

King Antiochus of Syria was not a Jew, and he was very cruel and unkind to the Jewish people. He wanted the Jews to worship the Greek god Zeus, and wouldn't let them worship their own god at their temple in Jerusalem.

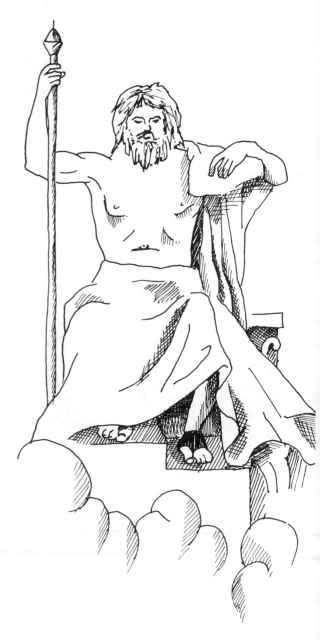

This made the Jews very angry, and they decided to fight the Syrian King. Even though they were greatly outnumbered they won their battle.

When they returned to their temple, they found that the army had made a terrible mess. So they had to clean it in order to make it holy once again.

They did this by re-lighting the temple's candle called a Menorah. This candle was really meant to burn all the time. They could only find one jar of oil to light the flame, and this they thought would only last for one day. But instead it kept the lamp burning for eight days and nights. And so Hanukkah celebrates this miracle.

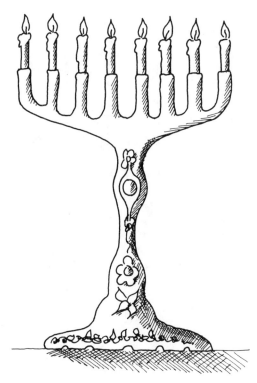

WHAT HAPPENS DURING HANUKKAH TIME?

The candle-lighting ceremony takes place in the evening, usually before the evening meal. This meal alway includes fried foods, and this often means pancakes or Potato Latkes. The oil used to fry these traditional pancakes is a reference to the cleaning and re-dedication of the temple in Jerusalem.

On the first night, Jewish families gather around the Menorah, or eight-branched candle stick, while one candle is lit. On the second night, two candles are kindled, and so on, until the eighth night. At this time two blessings are recited, and then the lighted Menorah is placed in a window so that everyone can see it and rejoice together.

For children, the highlight of the evening comes when they receive Hanukkah gelt, or presents of money, and gather around in a circle to play with a **dreidel**.

WHAT IS A DREIDEL?

A dreidel is a tiny spinning top with a different Hebrew letter printed on each of its four sides. Each letter has a different value in nuts or money.

DREIDEL GAME

Each child starts with the same number of nuts (or counters) and there is a pool of nuts in the centre. The children take turns to spin the top and take the value of the letter. The one with the most nuts or money at the end of the game, wins.

Nun	Nothing happens
Gimel	Take the nuts in the pool
Hay	Take half the nuts in the pool
Shin	Put one nut into the pool.

THINGS TO DO

A DREIDEL MOBILE

YOU WILL NEED

Large white cardboard, glue, cotton, potatoes for printing (cut into the Hebrew letters), paint, Hebrew letters cut out from paper.

METHOD

1. Cut out a large dreidel shape, making the border at least 8 cm (3") wide and remove the middle section. Potato print the border.

2. Cut out smaller dreidel shapes and paint. When they are dry, stick on the Hebrew letters.

3. Thread the smaller dreidels with cotton and hang in the middle of the main dreidel. This in turn can be threaded and hung up.

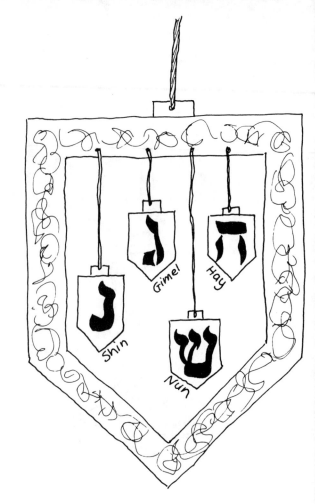

A SPINNING DREIDEL

YOU WILL NEED

Thin card 15 cm x 20 cm (6" x 8"), cut-out Hebrew letters, kebab stick at least 18 cm (7") long.

METHOD

1. Cut out a shape in the card as shown.

2. Fold along the dotted line and decorate the dreidel. First, make a small hole for the kebab stick in the top square and glue to the other four squares. Then glue the triangles. Insert the stick through the dreidel.

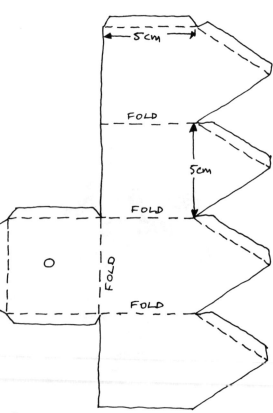

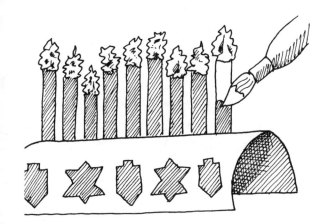

A   MENORAH

YOU WILL NEED

Large cardboard roll, 9 thin candles or candle shapes cut out from cardboard, paint. coloured paper.

METHOD

1. Cut out dreidel and Star of David shapes from the paper.

2. Remove a section along the length of the roll so that it doesn't roll over. Make nine slits along the top for the candles and paint.

3. If using cardboard candles, paint these white with yellow flames.

4. When the paint has dried, glue on the dreidel and star shapes. Place the candles in the slits.

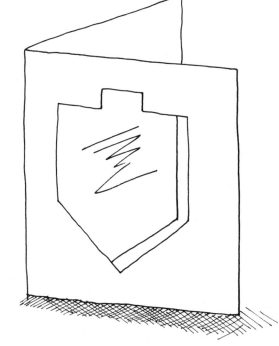

HANUKKAH CARDS

Make these by cutting out dreidel, Star of David or menorah shapes. Note that Hanukkah has other accepted spellings: Hannukkah, Chanukah, and Chanucah.

COOKING

POTATO LATKES

<u>YOU WILL NEED</u>

50 g (2 oz) self-raising flour or fine matzomeal
6 medium sized potatoes
1 teaspoon salt, pepper
2 eggs   Oil for deep frying

<u>METHOD</u>

1. Peel and finely grate the potatoes into a bowl of cold water to stop them going black. Leave for five minutes then strain through a muslin bag or squeeze as much liquid out as possible.

2. Mix all the ingredients to a thick batter. Heat the oil and drop in tablespoons of the mixture to make pancakes of about 8 cm (3") across . Fry on both sides until nicely brown.

Variation

Replace potato with grated carrot, onion or courgettes. If you are using courgettes add another two teaspoons of flour or fine matzomeal.

APPLE SAUCE

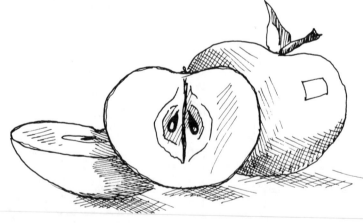

<u>YOU WILL NEED</u>

450 g (1lb) cooking apples
1 tablespoon water
1 teaspoon lemon juice
apple juice

<u>METHOD</u>

1. Peel, core and slice the apples and put in the saucepan with all the other ingredients and cover with a lid.

2. Place on a medium heat and bring to the boil. Reduce the heat and simmer for 10-15 minutes. Serve with the Latkes.

BUTTER BISCUITS (KUCHLICH)

YOU WILL NEED

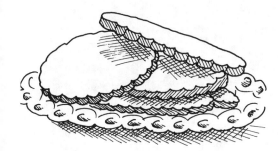

225 g (8 oz) self-raising flour
150 g (5 oz) margarine
75 g (3 oz) sugar
2 medium sized eggs
pinch of salt
grated rind of a lemon

Oven temperature: 170 'C/325 'F/Gas 3

METHOD

1. Sieve the flour with the salt and rub in margarine. Add sugar and mix well.

2. Beat eggs until frothy and add to mixture. Add lemon rind.

3. Knead and roll out to 1/2 cm thickness. Cut into rounds or special shapes. Place on a greased tin and bake until brown.

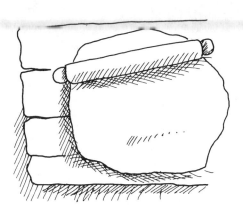

Suggested Songs: **A Song of Always, For Hanukkah, Dreidel Song**, from **Harvest of Holidays**, published by Cromwell-Collier, New York.

Hanukkah, One Little Candle, from **A Musical Calender Of Festivals**, published by Ward Lock Educational.

Spinning Top S'Vivon, Chanukah, Potato pancakes L'Vivot, from **Festivals (All the Year)**, by Jean Gilbert published by Oxford University Press.

Hanukkah Melodies, available from J.F.N. Publishing Co, Harold Poster House, Kingsbury Circle, London NW9 9SP.

KWANZAA

WHAT IS KWANZAA?

Kwanzaa is an African-American, non-religious festival which celebrates the harvest of the first crops. It is sometimes spelled Kwanza, and comes from a phrase which means first fruits in Swahili, an East African language. It was founded by a man called Maulana Karenga in 1966.

The Black community celebrates Kwanzaa during the period December 26th to January 1st but it is not a Black Christmas. It is a coming together of all the people and nations in Africa, and emphasizes the traditional spirit of all Africans.

Swahili is the language of Kwanzaa and was chosen because it is non-ethnic and is used by many of the nations of Africa.

THE NGUZO SABA (The seven principles which are observed on each of the days)

Day 1   Umoja (unity)
Day 2   Kujichagulia (self-determination)
Day 3   Ujima (collective work and responsibility)
Day 4   Ujamaa (co-operative economics)
Day 5   Nia (purpose)
Day 6   Kuumba (creativity)
Day 7   Imani (faith)

KWANZAA SYMBOLS

Mazao   (crops) fresh fruits and vegetables.

Mkeka   (place mat) all the symbols are placed on a mat, and this forms the foundation.

Kinara   (the candle holder for seven candles) one black candle is placed in the centre, three red, placed to the left, and three green placed to the right.

Vibunzi   (ears of corn) representing the number of children in the family or home.

Kikombe Cha Saba   (community unity cup which is used to sip drink in honour of ancestors and to reinforce family unity.

Mishumaa Saba   (the seven candles) representing the seven principles.

THINGS TO DO

KWANZAA CARDS

The official Kwanzaa colours are black which represents the people, red is for the struggle and blood shed, and green is for the youth and the future. Messages written in the cards should uphold the concept, meaning and practice of Kwanzaa. Their representations must be non-religious with strong positive African-American images.

By making and talking about each of the symbols the children will develop a greater understanding of what it means to share and care for each other.

A large collage can be made showing all the symbols and can be used for discussion.

COOKING

KARAMU (feast)

The night of the Karamu (feast) falls on December 31st. It is a time for families to share and enjoy a variety of food dishes, music and dance. During the feast a time is set aside for remembering, reassessment and recommitment. The feast is concluded with a farewell statement and a call for greater unity in the Black struggle.

GROUNDNUT STEW

This chicken dish in a rich peanut sauce is eaten widely all over Africa. It may be served with rice, fufu, or boiled cassava (tropical yucca).

YOU WILL NEED

1 kilo (3 lbs) chicken portions
110 g (4 oz) peanut butter
2 large onions, peeled and finely chopped
1 medium can tomatoes, blended or sieved
1 tablespoon tomato purée
1/2 teaspoon chilli powder
2 bay leaves
1 tablespoon of oil

METHOD

1. Remove the skin from the chicken portions. Place the chicken, oil, onions, salt and bay leaves in a large pan. Cover with a lid and cook gently for 5 minutes.

2. Pour in 470 ml (1pt) water and bring to the boil. Stir in the peanut butter and chilli powder. Cover and cook for a further 15 minutes.

3. Add the blended tomatoes and tomato purée. Stir, then cover and simmer for 45 minutes.

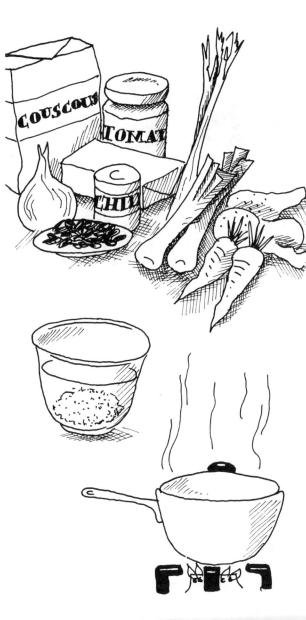

COUSCOUS

Couscous, made from wheat, is a fine semolina which has been mixed with water and made into small pellets. This is North Africa's national dish.

YOU WILL NEED

200 g (7 oz) couscous
25 g (1 oz) margarine
50 g (2 oz) raisins
1 onion, peeled and sliced
2 carrots, peeled and sliced
2 stalks of celery, scrubbed and chopped
2 chicken portions
2 leeks, cleaned
1 tablespoon tomato purée
1/2 teaspoon chilli powder, salt and pepper

METHOD

1. Soak the couscous in a bowl with 300 ml warm water for 10 minutes. Meanwhile prepare the vegetables, except the leeks. Place the vegetables and chicken in a large pan, and just cover with water. Bring to the boil, and cover the pan with a lid and turn down the heat. Simmer for 30 minutes.

2. Make a slit down the length of the leeks and wash away any soil, then cut into chunks. Add the tomato purée, raisins, leeks, chilli, salt and pepper to the stew. Stir well and continue cooking.

3. Cook the couscous by steaming it above the level of the boiling stew. Place the couscous in a metal sieve or colander lined with muslin, and fit into the top of the saucepan. Steam for 20-30 minutes with the lid on top. Make sure that the liquid from the stew does not touch the steamer as the couscous will become lumpy. Stir the couscous with a fork before turning it out on to a large warmed plate. Dot with pieces of margarine. Make a well in the centre and spoon in the meat and vegetables.

JANUARY

' January brings the snow
Makes our feet and fingers glow.'

January is nature's resting time. Much of the countryside is brown and bare, and many of the trees have lost their leaves. Nothing much grows, and it is hard for animals and birds to find food, especially if they live in open countryside and are not in the safety of hibernation. Birds of all kinds are to be seen going about in flocks eagerly searching for food. Many animals change the colour of their coats during the winter months. Hares, foxes and squirrels lose their ruddy tint and become much greyer. In that way they blend into the wintry landscape. In the north of Britain, the Mountain Hare becomes as white as the snow that covers the ground. In the coldest weather, cattle and sheep are kept inside. They are fed on the hay and silage which has been stored in the spring. In the garden, primroses, snowdrops and yellow jasmine can be found.

The word January comes from the name of a Roman god, Janus, who was the patron of births. Imagine a strange figure: a god with two faces. A god who looks forward and who looks back. He carries a key in his left hand. This is Janus. The Romans worshipped him in a temple that was kept open during war, and closed in times of peace. The Romans regarded him as the protector of their gates and doorways. His temple had twelve doors in it, each representing a month in the year. Through a gate there is both a going and a coming in. And so Janus became god of Beginnings and Ends.

NEW YEAR PAST AND PRESENT

'Last night, while we were fast asleep,
The old year went away.
It can't come back again because
A new one's come to stay.'

The traditions of January are connected with the old winter festivities celebrated in Scandinavia long ago. These usually involved the amount of time it was light, and were thought to encourage the sun to return. In some parts of Scotland and Northumberland there are still parades in the streets with lighted torches.

The giving of presents on New Year's Day is a time-old custom which has now almost entirely dropped out. Inspired by the idea of a **fresh start**, some people mark it by making resolutions.

In Brazil and Chile, the children receive presents on New Year's Eve. Brazilian children leave their shoes out on the window-sill the night before, just as elsewhere, stockings are hung up on Christmas Eve.

In China, some people have a fear of bad spirits, so they first sweep up all the dirt from their homes, in which the bad spirits like to live. Then they tip it beside a rope which has been tied round a tree, to make a large loop. Finally, they jump through the loop several times. The bad spirits come out of the dirt and try to follow, but soon get confused, and give up the chase.

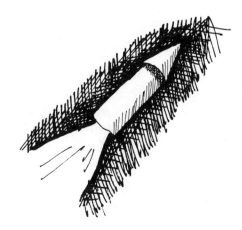

In Denmark, at midnight, young people knock on the doors of friends in masks and set off fireworks.

In England, crowds gather in Trafalgar Square in London, link arms, and at the stroke of midnight they sing **Auld Lang Syne**. This song was written by Scotland's national poet, Robert Burns (1759-96).

In Germany, an old New Year custom was to drop lumps of hot, molten lead in a bucket or barrel of cold water. As the pieces of lead cooled and hardened, people examined their shape. A round ring signified a wedding. If they thought the lead looked like a ship, this foretold a journey.

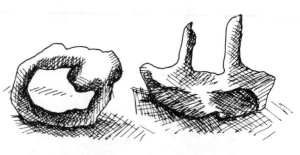

In Greece, New Year's Day is also the Festival of St Basil. He was well known for his kindness, and for many Greek children he is their Father Christmas. The children leave their shoes by the fireplace when they go to bed on New Year's Eve, hoping St Basil will fill the shoes with gifts.

In Holland, many people burn Christmas trees on street bonfires and let off fireworks.

In Hungary, this night is called **Silvester Night** and sometimes a young pig is let loose in the house. Everybody chases it, and whoever succeeds in touching its tail is supposed to have a lucky year.

In Israel, **Rosh Hashanah** is the Jewish New Year and is celebrated on two days in September or early October. It is celebrated by Jews all over the world. The day is marked by the blowing of the **shofar** (ram's horn) which calls the people to prayer.

In India, New Year is celebrated on March 22nd and is celebrated at different times according to which part of India you are in.

In Iran, people celebrate the New Year or **No-Ruz** on March 31st. It celebrates the first day of spring.

In Italy, the streets are found littered with old things, because people believe that in order to let something new in, you have to throw something old out.

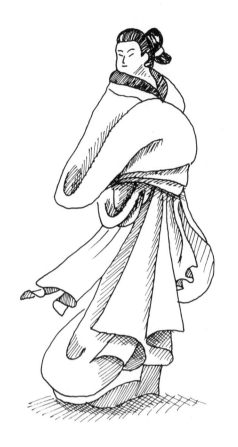

In Japan, New Year's Day is called **Shogatsu**. At midnight the temple bell is rung 108 times, one for each of the 108 sins. The sins are thus driven out, and the New Year can be started with a clean slate. They also hang a rope called a **shimenawa** (it is made from rice straw and decorated with strips of white cloth) across the front of their homes, to keep out evil spirits. In the morning, everyone dresses in Kimonos and drinks a toast with sake. New Year's breakfast is **ozoni**, a thick soup of vegetables and rice cake. All the children are given money in small envelopes which are tied with red and white ribbon and the children are often dressed in red and white. Many dishes are red and white which are lucky colours. Red and white fish cakes, tied into knots, white turnips rolled with red salmon, and there is always **seki-han**, red rice made by simmering white rice with red aduki beans.

KURI KINTON A Japanese dish for New Year

<u>YOU WILL NEED</u>

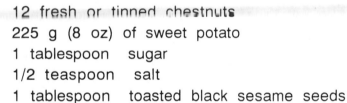

12 fresh or tinned chestnuts
225 g (8 oz) of sweet potato
1 tablespoon   sugar
1/2 teaspoon   salt
1 tablespoon   toasted black sesame seeds

<u>METHOD</u>

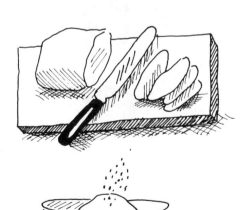

1. If you are using fresh chestnuts, soak them overnight in water, then peel them. Cover and simmer for 20 minutes until soft.

2. Peel the sweet potato and cut into small slices. Soak in water for at least 30 minutes. Cook in boiling water for 15-20 minutes until tender, then drain, season with sugar and salt, and mash.

3. Stir the cooked chestnuts into the mash. When the mixture is cool, mould into chestnut shapes and serve; or just make mounds in small bowls. Sprinkle a few sesame seeds on top.

NEW YEAR IN JAPAN

Every New Year in Japan, we (Japanese) celebrate. We call it **Oshogatsu**. On that day we children get money from our parents or relatives. It's called **Otoshidama**. On that day we eat special foods like **Ozoni**. It contains ricecake, some Japanese mushrooms, carrots, sometimes chicken. We also might eat other special foods like **Kamaboko** made from fish, or **Kuriton** made from chestnuts and many more. There are even special clothes and games. Some people wear **Kimono** on New Year's Day. Kimono is the special clothing for New Year. The games are called **Sugoroko**, **Takoagay**, **Hanetsuki** and **Comamawashi**. **Sugoroko** is played indoors. It's just a bit like snakes and ladders. **Takoagay** is just like kites. **Hanetsuki** is played outdoors. It's like badminton. **Comamawashi** is a game to spin tops and the one who lasts the longest is the winner.

by Tomo 13yrs old

Suggested Songs: **Oshogatsu (Till the New Year's Here)**, from **A Musical Calender of Festivals**, published by Ward Lock Educational.

In Russian homes you will find New Year Trees. This is the highlight of the Soviet winter season. Dyed Maroz, Grandfather Frost, brings toys to good boys and girls. It is said that he comes from the far north and moves so quickly, that no one ever sees him.

In Scotland, New Year's Eve is called **Hogmanay**. It is said that if the first person to cross the threshold in the New Year is a tall dark stranger, then the household will have good luck that year.

The children used to go **guising**. They sooted their faces and dressed in large sheets. The sheets were doubled up in front so as to form a vast pocket in which to hold their gifts and goodies. They would go along the streets in little bands, calling at the doors for an expected dole of oaten-bread or a slice of Black Bun.

The children, on coming to the door, would cry:

'Hogmanay
Trollalay!
Get up, good housewife, and shake your feathers,
And dinna think that we are beggars;
For we are bairns come out to play,
Get up and gie's our hogmanay.
My feet's cauld, my shoon's thin;
Gie' ma cakes, and let me rin.'

They often left a piece of coal behind them, as it is considered unlucky to visit any house empty-handed. Today people still visit friends and neighbours on Hogmanay, carrying a gift.

BLACK BUN

<u>YOU WILL NEED</u>

For the pastry

350 g (12 oz) plain flour
175 g (6 oz) butter
a little cold water, to mix

For the filling

450 g (1 lb) raisins
450 g (1 lb) currants
110 g (4 oz) crystallized peel
225 g (8 oz) plain flour
75 g (3 oz) almonds, blanched and chopped
50 g (2oz) brown sugar
1 teaspoon ground ginger
1 teaspoon ground cinnamon
1/2 teaspoon baking soda
1 teaspoon grated nutmeg
3 eggs   1-2 tablespoons milk
1 tablespoon brandy or whisky (optional)

Oven temperature: 180 'C/350 'F/Gas 4

<u>METHOD</u>

1. Rub together the flour and butter in a bowl to crumb texture then add enough water to make a dough.

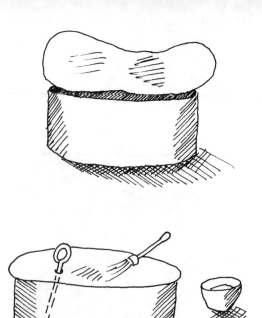

2. Roll the pastry out thinly and use this to line a greased 20 cm (8") cake tin and to make a pastry lid.

3. Mix together all the dry ingredients for the filling. Beat the eggs and milk together and stir most of this into the dry mixture to bind it. Leave some liquid aside for brushing the top. Add the brandy or whisky if desired.

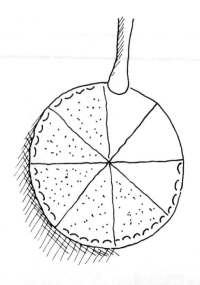

4. Put the mixture into the tin, smooth the surface, moisten the edges of the pastry lid and cover the top. Pierce right down to the bottom of the cake in several places with a skewer. Brush with a little beaten egg. Bake for about 3 hours.

PETTICOAT TAILS

This is a thinner, crisper version of the traditional Scottish shortbread.

<u>YOU WILL NEED</u>

110 g (4 oz) butter
75 g (3 oz) icing sugar
200 g (7 oz) plain flour

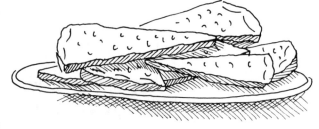

Oven temperature: 170 'C/325 'F/Gas 3

<u>METHOD</u>

1. Cream the butter with a wooden spoon and gradually beat in the icing sugar. Add all the flour and knead the mixture to form a smooth dough.

2. Grease a baking tray and place the dough on this. Roll out to form a circle. Then press out with your fingers to make a thin round 25 cm (10") in diameter. Cut round a large dinner plate if you want a smooth finish. Mark the top into 8 portions by scoring lightly with a knife.

3. Mark the edges into notches with the handle of a knife. Prick the top all over with a fork. Bake for 20-25 minutes until golden in colour. Leave to cool on the tin. Cut into fans to serve.

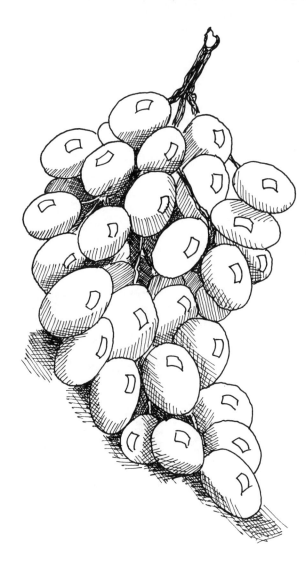

In Spain, it is believed that the luck of the coming year is settled by what happens on New Year's Day. It is thought that if you have plenty of good food to eat, you will have a prosperous year. Also it is traditional to eat a grape for every stroke of the clock at midnight on New Year's Eve.

In Vietnam, New Year or **Tet**, usually falls in February. Long bamboo poles are set up, decorated with leaves, feathers, tiny bells, little fishes, gold and silver papers, branches of cactus, and a lantern. At midnight people offer thanks for the benefits they received during the old year. A leafy branch covered with fruit and flowers is placed in the home. These are symbols of a happy and prosperous year to come.

Vietnamese people, like the Chinese, believe in a **kitchen** god. This god, according to mythology, travels to heaven on the back of a large carp and reports on how the family has behaved during the year. Some Vietnamese households still honour this tradition by buying a carp a few days before the start of the **Tet** festival. They place it in a large bowl of water before the family shrine, releasing it into a local river or pond on the first day of the festival. They also believe, like the Scots, that the character of the first person to step across the threshold of their homes, at the start of the festival, will influence their lives for the coming year. Another of their New Year customs is to make paper money and burn it, as an offering to their ancestors in heaven.

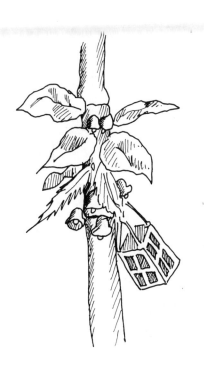

THINGS TO DO

JANUS MASK

Draw two profiles facing different directions on a piece of cardboard OR draw a face either side of a paper bag and make slits for the eyes.

FORCING BUDS INDOORS

You can **force** buds to open in winter or early spring.

<u>YOU WILL NEED</u>

Twigs with buds from any of the following:

Horse Chestnut, Birch, Willow, or Forsythia.

<u>METHOD</u>

Cut the twigs with pruning shears. Don't break them! Place twigs in water in a light spot indoors, then wait for the buds to open in a few weeks' time.

Suggested Songs: **January, February** (a song from South Africa), from **Songs that Children Sing**, by Eleanor Chroman, published by Oak Publications, New York. **Auld Lang Syne**, from **A Musical Calender of Festivals**, published by Ward Lock Educational.

ALL ABOUT THE WORM

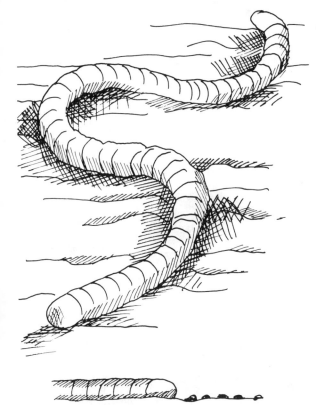

A story to read

If you touch the skin of an earthworm its body feels smooth, but it really has lots of tiny stiff bristles. These bristles help the worm to crawl and burrow deep into the ground. If you look closely you can see how its boneless body is divided into a number of rings. Those in front are larger than those in the middle.

The earthworm doesn't have ears and eyes, but it is very sensitive to light, and that's why it hides in the earth.

It doesn't have a jaw, just a mouth. Can you feel your own jaw and imagine what it would be like without a bone there? The worm eats its food through a muscular tube running right through its body. It is like the top end of a straw that has been made wiggly.

The worm eats soil and leaves small deposits called **casts** on the ground.

Did you know that earthworms can be both male and female? They lay their eggs in an oval cocoon which the worm leaves behind in the soil. Each cocoon is about the size of a grain of wheat. After a few weeks the young worms are hatched.

Worms living on land are eaten by birds, moles, badgers, hedgehogs, frogs and toads. In some parts of the world they are even eaten by people!

If worms are cut into two by a spade, their bodies will grow again.

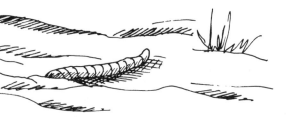

Next time you are in a garden, why not look for some worms?

Worms live in all types of environments. They can be found in the seas, earth, furniture and even in humans.

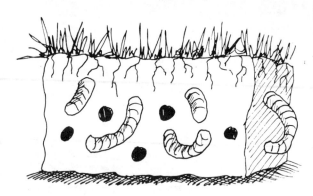

Charles Darwin, a British biologist (1809-1882), estimated that an acre of garden has on average about 53,000 earthworms, through which some 10 tons of soil are passed.

MAKE A WORMERY

One of the best ways to create a wormery is to use and old fish tank.

YOU WILL NEED

Potting compost, sand and earth, stones, grass or grass seeds, black paper, worms, gauze or glass to cover.

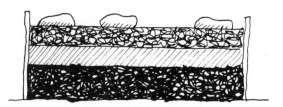

METHOD

1. Fill the tank with different layers, 8 cm (3") deep, of compost, sand and earth. Arrange the stones around the tank and add the worms.

2. Plant the grass at the top or use a layer of turf. Feed the worms with leaves, carrots, apples, dead insects and snails.

3. Keep the tank covered with a piece of gauze or a sheet of glass with a small space for ventilation. This will allow air to circulate, while keeping the worms in.

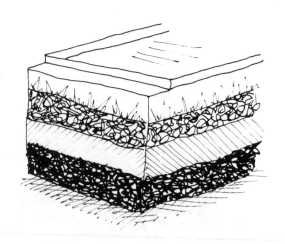

4. Position the wormery in a cool, dark place and water the soil now and again. Keep it only as long as is necessary for observation.

A poem which is told by a bird   Anon

Nobody likes me,
Everybody hates me,
I think I'll go and eat worms.
Big fat squishy ones,
Little thin skinny ones,
See how they wriggle and squirm.

Bite their heads off,
Schlurp! they're lovely,
Throw their tails away.
Nobody knows,
How big I grow,
On worms three times a day.

CHINESE NEW YEAR

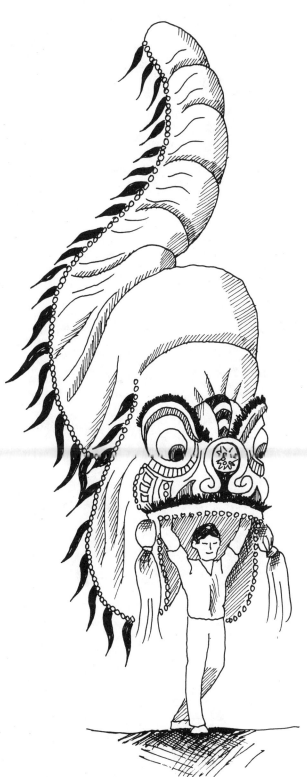

The old Chinese calender is different from the Western calender. It is based on the movement of the moon. Each time a new moon appears, a new month begins. This makes the Chinese year ten days shorter than the Western year, which is based on the movements of the sun. The moon-based year is called a **lunar** year and the sun-based year a **solar** year. The difference between the two kinds of years is made up by adding an extra month to the lunar year every two or three years. The date of New Year changes every year, but it always falls between January 21st and February 20th

Preparation for the festival begins at least ten days before the event. People clean out their homes and shops. Special fairs are held each evening to sell flowers, paintings, drawings, and crockery.

On New Year's Eve, all the family gather together at home to see in the New Year. Outside, the celebrations begin on the stroke of midnight. Fireworks explode in the streets to frighten away the spirits of the old year.

The lily is the symbol of the Chinese New Year. The legend says that if the lily plant blooms and grows well, you shall have a prosperous year. But if the lily doesn't bud, bad luck will be in store.

Today, in the Chinese areas of London, and in other large cities, the local Chinese people celebrate the New Year with processions through the streets. These are led by friendly dragons which knock on each door to bring good luck.

Each Chinese year carries the name of an animal. According to the legend, twelve animals answered a call from Buddha. These were the rat, ox, tiger, rabbit, dragon, snake, horse, ram, monkey, cockerel, dog and pig.

THE LEGEND OF THE ANIMALS

A story to read

A long time ago there were twelve animals, a rat, an ox, a tiger, a rabbit, a dragon, a snake, a horse, a ram, a monkey, a cockerel, a dog, and last but not least, a pig. One day all the animals were arguing. They wanted every year to have one of their names, and each one of them wanted to be first.

"**This year should be called after me**" barked the dog.

"**No!**" hissed the snake, "**It should be called after me.**"

"**No!**" roared the tiger, "**After me.**"

And so they argued all day. The gods, on hearing this rumpus, ordered the animals to stop. The dog stopped, the snake stopped, the tiger stopped, and they all stood in silence and listened.

"**Can you see that river over there?**" asked one of the gods.

"**Yes,**" replied the animals. "**Then I want you all to race across and I will name the first year after the winner**" said the god.

All the animals lined up and on the orders of the god, the great race began. The ox was very strong, and was soon leading, but the rat was clever and grabbed hold of the ox's tail and climbed up onto its back. The ox did not even know that the rat was there and felt sure that he was going to win. Just as the ox reached the other side of the river, the rat ran along its back, down its nose and jumped off onto the land.

"**Hoorah!**" shouted the rat, "**I am the winner**."

The ox was very surprised and could not understand how the rat had managed to reach the end first. The gods laughed and declared the rat really was the winner, and that this year should be the year of the rat. The ox came next, followed by the tiger, the hare, the dragon, the snake, the horse, the ram, the monkey, the cockerel, the dog, and last of all, the pig.

You can work out your birth sign from the following guidelines. The Chinese New Year has a twelve-year cycle and starts late January or early February. So if you are born on the 10th January 1985, your birth sign is the Rat.

The Rat	1984	The Horse	1990
The Ox/Buffalo	1985	The Ram/Goat	1991
The Tiger	1986	The Monkey	1992
The Hare/Cat/Rabbit	1987	The Cockerel/Rooster	1993
The Dragon	1988	The Dog	1994
The Snake	1989	The Pig	1995

Suggested Songs: **How Yee Gaw Suey Sin Fah (Chinese Lily song)**, from **Songs That Children Sing**, by Eleanor Chroman, published by Oak Publications, New York.

New Year Greeting, from **A Musical Calender of Festivals**, published by Ward Lock Educational.

Merry have we met, Boat Song, Chinese New Year, Feng Yang Song, from **Festivals (all the year)**, by Jean Gilbert, published by Oxford University Press.

THE FEAST OF LANTERNS

On the third day of the celebration held during the Chinese New Year comes the Feast of Lanterns. Lanterns of various shapes, colours and sizes are hung in gardens, on porches, in streets and in temples.

People come out into the streets carrying lighted lanterns and join the parade, which is led by a huge dragon. The dragon is a symbol of goodness and strength. It is a great empty shell made of bamboo covered with silk or paper and painted. Men walk inside the dragon only showing their feet. Crowds gather to watch the parade.

THINGS TO DO

A CHINESE LANTERN

<u>YOU WILL NEED</u>

A4 paper, glitter and crayons, glue.

<u>METHOD</u>

1. Colour the paper. Fold in half lengthwise and draw lines 8 cm (3") and 2 cm (1") wide. Cut along the lines and sprinkle with glitter

2. Stick the edges of the lantern together. Make the handle with a strip of coloured paper.

A DRAGON'S HEAD

Take a cardboard box big enough to fit over a child's head. Cut out the dragon's eyes, and paint. Use crêpe paper to make a flowing mane.

MASKS

The children can make masks either depicting the animal for that year or they can do their own year sign. (See page 81)

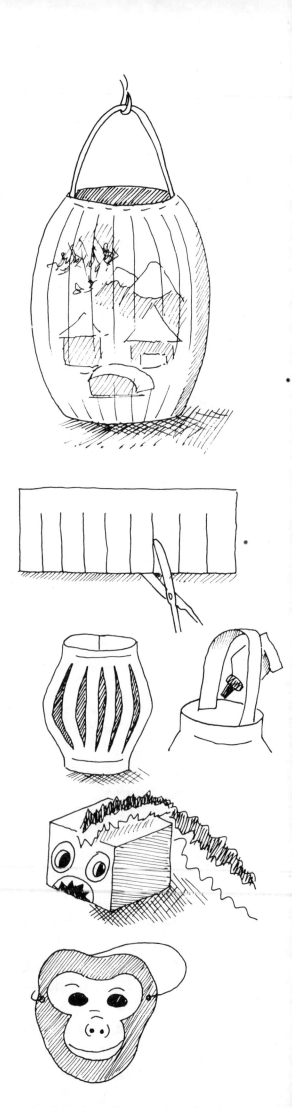

A CHINESE DRAGON

YOU WILL NEED

Long balloon, newspaper, egg boxes, glue, paint, card.

METHOD

1. Mix the glue in a large bowl. Tear paper into strips, paste and place around the balloon. Allow to dry over several days.

2. Cut out a dragon's head and four feet from the card and paint.

3. Balance the balloon by slicing a little off the bottom. Then cut out the cup shapes from the egg carton and glue these on the dragon's back and paint. Allow to dry.

Make a slit at the end of the balloon and slot in the body

Make two slits either side of the body and slot in the feet.

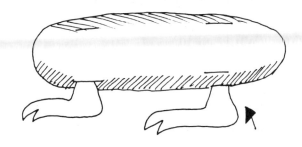

A DRAGON FRIEZE

Cut out a large dragon shape, then sponge paint it. Once dry, stick on crêpe and shiny paper. Use an egg carton for the eyes. Glue egg carton shapes along the back.

As the Chinese paint with a fine brush and ink, perhaps the children can make their own pictures using these materials.

COOKING

The kitchen is an important place at Chinese New Year. At this time, families worship **Tsao-Shen** (the god of the kitchen). During the week before the festival, this god is believed to go up to heaven and report on the conduct of each member of the family during the past year. On New Year's Eve, the god will return, and the evening is celebrated with a special meal.

Food at this time includes bowls of peanuts, melon seeds, and preserved fruits. Each of these has a special significance such as good fortune, long life, and happiness. Another traditional food at this time is dumplings.

CHINESE DUMPLINGS

These dumplings can be filled with chopped pork, cabbage and spring onion, or whatever you choose, flavoured with ginger, soya sauce, salt, pepper and sesame oil. They are served with a mixture of vinegar and soya sauce.

YOU WILL NEED

2 cups flour
1 cup water
1/2 teaspoon filling

METHOD

1. Sift the flour with the salt and add the water gradually making the dough. Knead well and cover with a cloth. Prepare your filling.

2. Knead the dough again and break into small balls. Flattened into thin pancake rounds of about 5 cm (2"). Put 1/2 teaspoon of filling in one half of the pancake.

3. Wet the edges with water, fold over and press together to make a half-moon-shaped dumpling. Place in a steamer and cook for 10 minutes at high heat or boil in water for the same length of time.

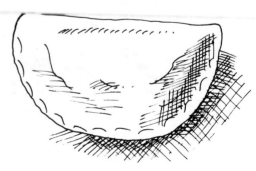

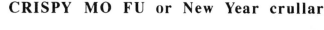

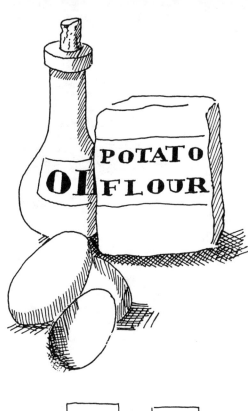

CRISPY MO FU or New Year crullar

YOU WILL NEED

225 g (8 oz) plain flour
110 g (4 oz) lard
oil for frying
salt to taste   4 eggs

METHOD

1. Mix the lard, flour and salt together in a bowl. When lumpy, whip the eggs and pour them into a well in the mixture. Knead the mixture for about 15 minutes.

2. Roll flat with a rolling pin and cut into small rectangular pieces of about 5 cm (2") long and 2 cm (1") wide. Make a slit down the middle and then turn them inside out. Deep fry the Mo Fu in oil.

NIAN-OAO (CHINESE NEW YEAR CAKE)

YOU WILL NEED

450 g (1 lb) brown sugar
450 g (1 lb) glutinous rice flour
a greased 20 cm (8") cake tin

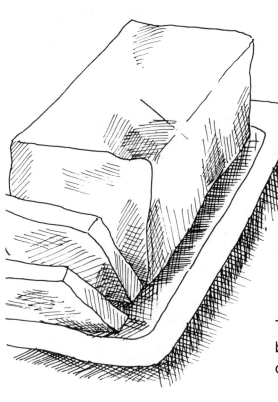

METHOD

1. Boil 300 ml (10 fl oz) of water. Take from the heat, and add sugar, mix until it becomes syrupy. Pour flour into a large bowl, and add the syrup a little at a time, stirring as you do so until smooth. Then pour the mixture into the cake tin.

2. Boil at least 1 litre (1 3/4 pt) of water in a large pot. Carefully place the cake tin on a steaming rack in the water. Cover the pot with a lid and steam for 2 hours, making sure that the water does not boil dry.

The Nian-oao will keep for weeks. In fact it tastes better the older it is. It can be re-steamed to eat hot or can be eaten cold as a sticky sweet snack.

NEW YEAR COOKIES

These New Year Cookies are a symbol of good luck.

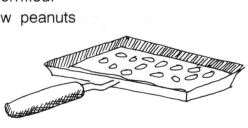

YOU WILL NEED

110 g (3 1/2 oz) margarine	110 g (3 1/2 oz) sugar
175 g (6 oz) rice flour	50 g (2 oz) cornflour
25 g (1 oz) dates (optional)	25 g (1 oz) raw peanuts
1 tablespoon sesame seeds	1 egg

Oven temperature: 180 'C/350 'F/Gas 4

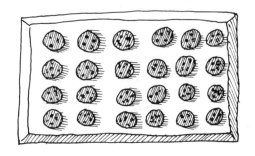

METHOD

1. Line a baking tray with greaseproof paper. Toast the peanuts and sesame seeds under the grill until golden in colour, and chop finely. Cream the margarine with the sugar until fluffy. Beat in the egg to form a dough, adding a little flour if the mixture shows signs of curdling.

2. Flour your hands then divide the mixture into 14 balls. Shape into cookies 8 cm in diameter and 1/2 cm (1/4") thick. If using dates press into the centre of each ball and fold over the dough. Shape into a cookie with no date showing. Bake on a tray for 12-15 minutes.

BEAN SPROUTS

YOU WILL NEED

50 g (2 oz) Mung beans, soaked overnight, a colander, lined and covered with a tea towel.

METHOD

Wash the beans, removing any that are damaged. Place in a jar or colander and find a place away from draught and sunlight. Keep the beans moist with warm water but don't drown them. Repeat every day for 3-5 days until the sprout are 5 cm (2") high. Remove any that go mouldy.

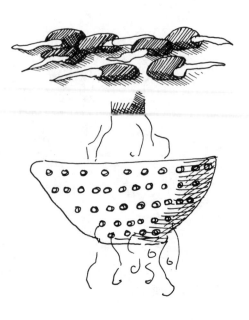

Home-grown Mung beans are greener than shop-bought beans which are grown in the dark.

FEBRUARY

'February brings the rain
Thaws the frozen lake again'.

February is still cold and wintry, but this won't last much longer. The snow is melting making the ground slippery and wet. Pastures are dressed with fertilizer to make the grass grow tall and strong.

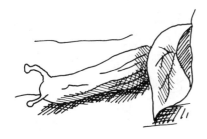

'All Nature seems at work,
Slugs leave their lair.
The bees are stirring.
Birds are on the wing,
And Winter slumbering
In the open air
Wears on his face
A dream of spring."

Julius Caesar made February the second month instead of the twelfth month. Until Caesar's time, February had thirty days. Caesar took one day to add to July, the month named after him. Then Augustus took another one to add to August, the month named after him, leaving February with only 28 days. February does however have an extra day every four years - every Leap Year - to keep the calendar exactly in time with the seasons.

The word February comes from the Latin Februarius, meaning **to purify**. The ancient Romans held a festival of purification to prepare for the year to come, and the name stuck to the month even after it was moved from twelfth to second in the calender.

The Romans regarded Februa as a festival for spiritual cleansing, but they celebrated the occasion by overeating.

ST BRIDE'S DAY

February 1st

St Bride is the patron saint of milkmaids. In Ireland where she was born, and also in the Isle of Man, she is always known as St Bridget.

THE STORY OF BRIDGET

<u>**A story to read**</u>

There was once a little girl called Bridget, who lived in Ireland. Bridget was very fond of birds. When she called them, they would come and sit on her hand and she would feed them bread crumbs. When she told them to fly away, they wouldn't go. They just circled around her, playing and singing.

One day her mother sent her milking with the other milkmaids. They were collecting milk in order to make butter. But Bridget didn't make butter from her milk, she gave it to the poor people. Her mother wasn't very happy about this.

While the other milkmaids started to make their butter, Bridget prayed very hard, and all of a sudden the butter began to grow and grow. Bridget was so happy that she gave away the extra butter. From this day Bridget became the patron saint of milkmaids.

As soon as she was old enough, Bridget became a nun (in fact, the first nun in Ireland). She built herself a little cell, which is a bit like a little house, under an oak tree. Her cell was called Kildara which means 'cell of the oak'. It wasn't long before other nuns came to join her, and soon the lonely little house became a great nunnery. Around this nunnery arose the city of Kildare.

WHAT DO BIRDS EAT?

Birds can eat a wide range of fruits. They also eat snails after breaking their shells. Spring caterpillars, insects and plenty of earthworms make a special treat. But during the bleak winter months, birds have a hard time finding food.

Birds such as tits, starlings, magpies, and crows can be offered mince or hanging bones with a little meat. Robins are especially fond of mealworms (the grubs of the beetle) which can be found in pet shops. Once you have got a supply they can be cultivated in an earthenware jar by filling it with bran, flour and dry bread. Fresh coconut is another favourite bird food.

THINGS TO DO

MAKING A BIRD CAKE

Make a hole either side of a margarine tub and thread with string. Fill with any of the following - chopped bacon rinds, tiny pieces of bread, raisins, sultanas, chopped apple, bird seed, cake or biscuit crumbs, and oatmeal. An adult must pour on some melted fat. Wait until it hardens before you hang it up.

Another way is to fill a vegetable net with un-salted peanuts, **or** thread peanuts on a string and hang them up. You must never give birds any salted food as they are unable to dispose of excess salt and this can prove fatal to small birds.

MAKING A BIRD TABLE

Use the base of a wooden vegetable box. Hammer a nail in each of the corners. Fix string to the nails and hang it from a tree.

TALKING ABOUT MILK

Ask the children to name animals that produce milk. All mammals produce milk - elephants, goats, sheep, buffalo, asses, reindeer, zebu, whales, camels, and humans.

Butter, yoghurt and cheese are made from milk.

MAKING YOGHURT

YOU WILL NEED.

570 ml (1 pint) of milk
1 tablespoon of bought natural yoghurt
a saucepan, a bowl and a clean towel

METHOD

1. The adult must heat the milk gently until bubbles appear. Allow to cool for at least half an hour.

2. Put the tablespoon of yoghurt into a bowl. Then stir in the milk gently. Ask the children to notice if the mixture is runny or firm.

3. Cover the bowl with the clean tea-towel and leave overnight in a warm place for the yoghurt to grow.

4. See if the children notice a difference in the mixture. You can flavour the yoghurt with fresh fruit. Some acid fruits like rhubarb may make it

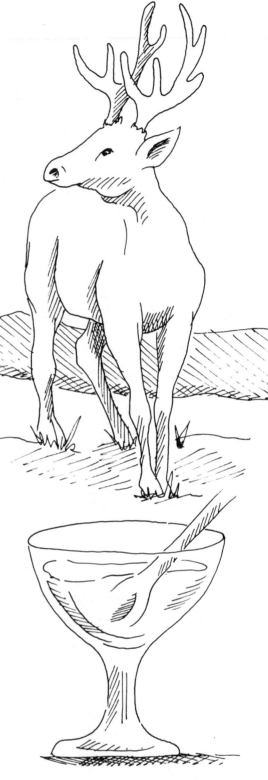

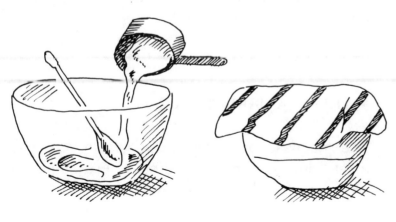

MAKING BUTTER

1. Take a fresh bottle of full fat milk and pour the cream from the top into a jar with a lid **or** use single cream.

2. Make sure the lid is on tight and then the children can shake it vigorously.

This can take some time so you can finish it off with an electric whisk. When the butter is made, you may like to make some bread to go with it.

THE COW

The friendly cow, all red and white,
I love with all my heart:
She gives me cream with all her might,
To eat with apple-tart.

She wanders lowing here and there,
And yet she cannot stray,
All in the pleasant open air,
The pleasant light of day:

And blown by all the winds that pass
And wet with all the showers,
She walks among the meadow grass
And eats the meadow flowers.

by Robert. L. Stevenson

Suggested Songs: **Morning Mr Blackbird**, from **Flying A Round**, published by A & C Black.

What the Birds Say, from **Infant Joy - A Complete Repertoire of Songs**, published by University of London Press.

Spring Birds' Nest, The Birds, from Rhyme and Rhythm, by Gibson and Wilson, published by Macmillan.

TU B'SHVAT FESTIVAL

February 2nd

Tu B'Shvat is the annual tree planting festival for children in Israel. On this day people plant trees in the forests and give money for trees. The children parade through the streets carrying gardening tools. They also sing, dance and play games.

The ceremonial tree planting recalls the story in the Talmud, which says that the Jewish ancestors planted trees when their children were born. When the children grew up the trunks or branches of the trees were used to make their wedding canopies or tents.

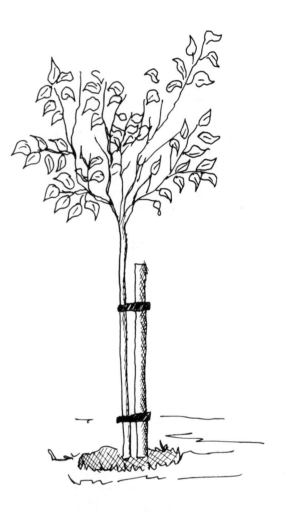

To celebrate this event it is customary to eat up to fifteen different kinds of fruits and nuts. Each represents a feature of Jewish life.

The children drink four cups of wine symbolizing the changes that nature undergoes in the four seasons. Both light and dark fruit juices are drunk, these being apple, orange, cranberry and dark grape juice.

THINGS TO DO

COUNTING FRUITS ACTIVITY

Collect as many different fruits as possible. One option is to cut pictures out of a magazine and make a collage. Ask the children to count the different fruits. Group them by skin type, or colour, and count the number in each group.

TOUCHING FRUITS ACTIVITY

With the fruits you have collected talk about hard and soft skins. Talk about different textures, rough and smooth.

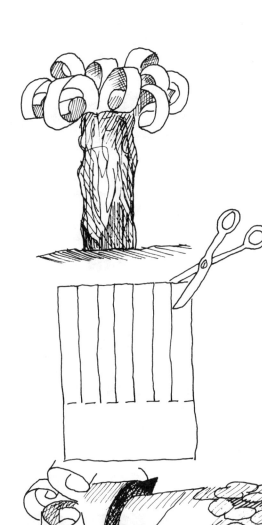

MAKING A PALM TREE

YOU WILL NEED

A4 paper, crayons, glue, scissors, an empty toilet roll, wood or pencil shavings.

METHOD

1. Draw a line 18 cm (7") below the top of the paper. Then from the top of the paper to the line draw lines at 2 cm (1") intervals, and colour this part green. Colour the rest brown. Cut along the lines. Then curl each cut strip by gently running each strip of paper between your thumb and scissors.

2. Glue the toilet roll, and wrap the brown section of paper round the roll. Then glue on the wood shavings to give a bark effect.

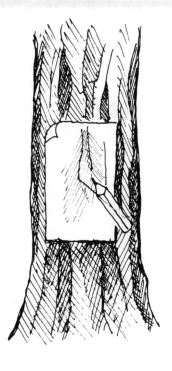

BARK RUBBINGS AND WOOD SHAVINGS

YOU WILL NEED

Large paper, crayons, different types of wood shavings from sawdust to large shavings, glue.

METHOD

Place a large piece of paper on a tree trunk and rub on it with a crayon. Then glue on different types of wood shavings.

GROWING PARSNIP AND CARROT TOPS

<u>YOU WILL NEED</u>

Parsnips and carrots with green tops, a tray filled with earth 10 cm (4") deep.

<u>METHOD</u>

1. Cut at least 2 cm (1") off the top of several parsnips and carrots.

2. Plant the tops in the tray. Water when required. In two weeks small green shoots will appear.

3. Measure the daily progress of the tops on a piece of paper.

MAKE YOUR OWN CHARCOAL

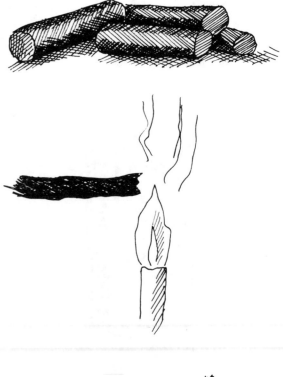

If wood is made to burn in insufficient air, it will smoulder, and turn into charcoal.

<u>YOU WILL NEED</u>

Long thin twigs, paper for drawing.

<u>METHOD</u>

1. Place the twigs in the oven for about an hour, allowing them to dry out and go black.

2. Take one twig and hold it over a naked flame for a few seconds. Blow out the flame and tap the end so that the fire is put out. Now the twig is ready to draw with. This comes out quite black. To get a lighter effect draw with the end of a match stick.

3. Paint with charcoal by completely burning the twigs until they turn into ash. Mix with a little water, then paint.

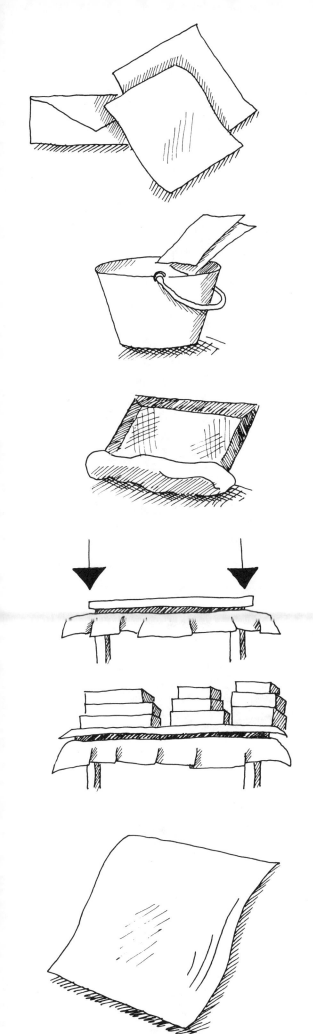

MAKING RECYCLED PAPER

Paper is traditionally made from tree pulp. However, the need to preserve the rain forest has made it important for children to understand about recycling.

YOU WILL NEED

Old newspaper, wire mesh, some absorbent cloths, 2 buckets or bowls, wooden spoon, powder paint (optional) , plastic bag (cut down the seams for safety), weights e.g. heavy books.

METHOD

1. Soak some old newspaper in a bucket overnight. Drain off the extra water and mash the paper with the wooden spoon into a pulp. Mix in the paint if you want coloured paper.

2. Put the pulp into another bowl and add an equal volume of water. Mix these together.

3. Slide the wire mesh into the mixture, lifting it out covered in pulp.

4. Lay a cloth on a flat surface. Place the mesh (with pulp side down) quickly and carefully onto the cloth.

5. Press down hard, remove the mesh, leaving the pulp on the cloth. Put another cloth on top and press down firmly.

6. Repeat steps 4, 5 and 6.

7. When this is done, place the plastic bag on the top and weight the pile down.

8. In a few hours (when the pulp has turned to paper), gently peel the paper off the cloths. Leave each piece on some newspaper until it is completely dry.

The paper should now be ready for use.

CANDLEMAS FESTIVAL

February 2nd

We didn't always have electric lights. Candles were used every day - not just for party cakes and special occasions! Candlemas takes its name from the blessing of candles on that day for use in church during the forthcoming year. Simeon spoke of Jesus Christ as **'A light to lighten the Gentiles'**. Candles are blessed in church, lit, and carried in procession. They are made in a host of attractive shapes and colours, and some of them will burn for many hours.

In past times people used leftover beef or mutton fat to make their own candles, with flax for wicks. Can you imagine the appalling smell when they began to smoulder!

CANDLE PICTURES

<u>YOU WILL NEED</u>

A candle, thin paint, paper.

<u>METHOD</u>

Draw a picture with your candle, then paint or sponge over it with thin paint and your picture will appear.

EGG EXPERIMENT

This is a demonstration using an egg and a candle which must be done by an adult.

Hold an egg close to the flame of a lit candle until it turns black all over. Submerge the egg in water - it will turn silver!

Suggested Songs: **Candlemas Eve**, from **A Musical Calender of Festivals**, published by Ward Lock Educational.

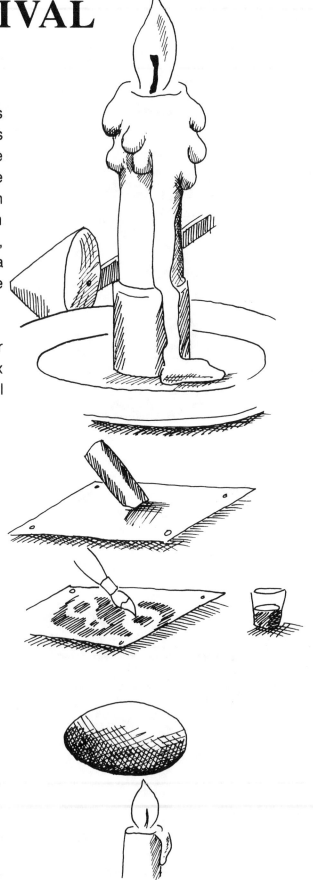

SETSUBUN FESTIVAL

February 3rd

Setsubun is a joyful Japanese festival. A hundred men or women, born in a year with the same sign as the current year, scatter lucky beans or rice-cake and the people who collect them will then receive good fortune.

Here is a story by a boy aged 13 from the Japanese school in London.

MY SETSUBUN by Yudai Shiratori

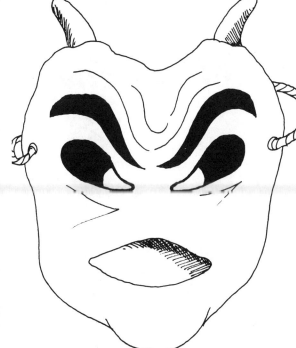

Setsubun is a festival on the third or fourth of February, the day separates Winter and Spring. To celebrate the new season, we scatter the beans outside, saying **'Get out the Evil, come in the Happiness'**. We throw the beans outside to hit the evil. Then if we eat as many beans as our age, we will have a healthy and good year.

When I was young, on Setsubun I always made a mask of a devil. Lots of children wore devil masks and we would throw beans at each other. All the shops sold Setsubun things (beans and masks) and we all had fun. I always ate many more beans than my age, and my parents only just managed to eat enough beans. My mother would often get some sweets too on Setsubun, and scatter them around in the house for us children to have. Setsubun was always fun and it was one of my favourite festivals.

BEAN ACTIVITIES

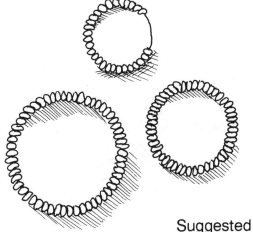

1. Place some cooked soya beans in a bowl, and ask the children to eat as many beans as their age.

2. Draw different circles. Using raw beans ask the children to glue as many as they can in each circle. Then count how many are in each circle.

Suggested Songs: **Planting Beans**, from **Rhyme and Rhythm** by Gibson and Wilson, published by Macmillan.

CARNIVAL AROUND THE WORLD

Carnival, meaning **farewell to the flesh** (from the Latin **carne vale**), was originally an old Italian festival which lasted from Twelfth Night after Christmas to Ash Wednesday. Lent begins on Ash Wednesday which can fall on any date between February 7th and March 9th.

Today Carnival takes many forms and is often planned months in advance.

The American city of New Orleans has celebrated this festival since the French students settled there in 1827. The first decorated floats appeared in 1837, and carnival parades became an annual event in 1857. The music of carnival is Jazz and there are band floats and street dancing.

In Austria, figures dressed as ghosts, witches and death appear in the carnival procession. They parade through the streets to the music of drums, whips and bull-roarers.

In Brazil, Rio hosts one of the most famous carnivals. The streets are decorated with huge clown and devil masks which are placed on standards or lamps posts. This 18-hour festival is filled with joy and colour. Twenty schools of **samba** compete in a song writing and dance contest. The samba schools put on a show revolving around a central theme, like events in history, famous people, or books.

England hosts the Notting Hill Carnival. The people who settled here from the West Indies brought with them this tradition. Every year since 1961, on the Summer Bank Holiday which falls on the last weekend in August, floats and brass steel bands have filled the streets of Notting Hill in West London. This is the first time that the traditional carnival has been celebrated away from Lent.

In both Germany and Switzerland, groups of masked actors go from house to house performing plays during carnival.

In Italy, carnival is celebrated in many different ways. In Venice it is celebrated by the people wearing colourful costumes and masks. In the processions in Rome, people throw flowers at each other. The throwing of flowers is part of an ancient fertility rite and carries the same idea of good luck as the throwing of rice or confetti at a wedding.

In Mexico there are colourful floats with actors performing plays about bandits and the triumph of good over evil.

In the South of France, the carnival or **Mardi Gras (Fat Tuesday)** is led by the **King of the Carnival**, a large straw man. He leads the merry-making with clowns, horses and colourful floats filled with beautiful flowers. In Meze Herault in France the procession of **Boef Gras (Fat Beef)**, is held. This is when animals are led through the streets by butchers in costume.

In Spain, castanets and guitars accompany dancing in the street. Also huge papier-mâché figures known as the **Gigantes y Cabezudos** (giants with big heads) appear in the carnival processions. They represent important historical characters. These figures originally represented the much older traditional theme of the Battle of Summer and Winter.

Trinidad and Tobago in the West Indies celebrate with a famous figure on stilts, known as Jab Jab or Jab Molassi. This is a devil with a long whip who is covered with molasses. The music of steel bands and Calypso fills the air and everyone makes lovely elaborate costumes. This three day carnival dates back to 1783 when French speaking immigrants arrived on the Island. Calypso songs play an important part in this carnival and have been sung for over 180 years.

EASTER PRETZEL

In Germany doughnuts and pretzels are eaten at carnival time. The very first pretzels are said to have been invented by a baker who lived at the foot of the Alps. He was thrown into prison because he had been supplying bad bread. He was told that he would only be freed on one condition. He had to bake something through which the sun would shine three times. And so after a lot of thought and many sleepless nights he came up with the pretzel.

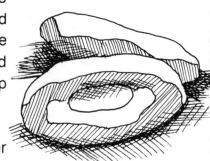

In some parts of Germany children are given enormous Easter Pretzels which are baked into heart-shapes, then decorated with ribbon streamers. The children carry the pretzels to their neighbour's house, singing: 'Winter heraus Sommer herein!'

COOKING

PRETZELS

<u>YOU WILL NEED</u>

225 g (8 oz) plain flour
50 g (2 oz) melted butter
25 g (1 oz) sugar
125 ml lukewarm milk
1 1/4 teaspoon dried yeast
1/4 teaspoon ground cinnamon
1 beaten egg, cooking oil, pinch salt

Oven temperature: 220 C/425 F/Gas 7

<u>METHOD</u>

1. Mix the dried yeast and sugar with the milk. Leave to stand in a warm place for 10 minutes. Stir the flour, salt and cinnamon into a bowl and make a well in the centre. Pour the yeast mixture into the well. Add the butter and half the beaten egg. Mix to a smooth dough and knead lightly for 3-4 minutes. Cover and leave to stand for 20 minutes.

2. With floured hands divide the mixture into eight. Roll each portion into a long sausage and fold each end into the centre. Leave to stand on a floured baking tray for a further 20 minutes. Brush with the remaining beaten egg. Bake near the top of the oven for about 20 minutes.

THREE BREAD ROLLS by Leo Tolstoy

A story to read

One day a peasant went to a fair. He was hungry, and so he bought a large bread roll and ate it. He was still hungry. So he bought a second bread roll and ate that. He was still hungry, so he bought a third bread roll and ate that.

Those three bread rolls had not been enough to satisfy him. Yes, he was still hungry. This time he bought a bag of pretzels. He ate one, and at last his hunger had gone. The peasant clapped his hands, and said "**Well, I never! What a fool I am. I ought to have eaten a pretzel in the first place because one little pretzel was all I needed**". And so he went home whistling.

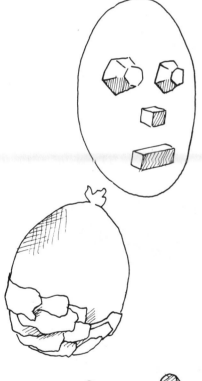

THINGS TO DO

MAKING MASKS

Paper Plate Masks

Decorate a large paper plate. Glue on egg cartons for the eyes and small cardboard boxes for the mouth and nose to make a three-dimensional face. Attach to a long stick.

Papier Mâché masks

Take a round balloon and cover it with layers of glue and strips of paper. Once it is dry cut it in half and cut out sections for the eyes, nose and mouth. The mask can now be painted or decorated.

MUSICAL INSTRUMENTS

SHAKERS

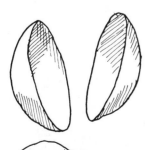

<u>YOU WILL NEED</u>

Rice, any dried pulses, buttons, or small stones, empty washing-up bottles, yoghurt cartons or any plastic container, paper, paint.

METHOD

Put different quantities of pulses in your plastic container to create different sounds. Cover the containers with paper and then paint.

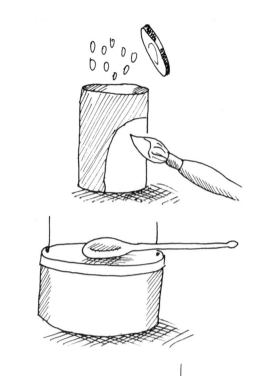

A DRUM

Take a coffee tin with a plastic lid and decorate it. Make a hole either side at the top, thread string through the holes and tie the ends together. Use a wooden spoon or dowel as a drumstick.

SANDPAPER SCRATCHER

Glue sandpaper onto two blocks of wood. Rub them together to make a sound.

CALABASHES

These are well known in Oyo, Nigeria, and are traditionally made out of a **gourd** which is a hard-shelled bulbous fruit like a cucumber. They are grown on vines. When ripe, the soft insides are scooped out, and the hard rinds are left to dry. Intricate designs are carved out on the outer surface.

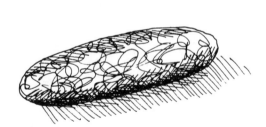

<u>YOU WILL NEED</u>

Newspaper, a long balloon, glue, dried pulses.

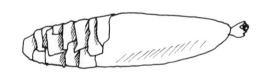

<u>METHOD</u>

1. Blow up the long balloon. Tear the newspaper into narrow strips. Paste and cover the balloon with at least five layers of paper. Try not to use too much glue. Allow to dry for at least 24 hours.

2. Cut a small hole at the top of the balloon, and pour in some dried pulses until you are happy with the sound it makes. Cover the hole with several layers of paper. Paint the Calabash, and when it is dry, apply a thin coat of varnish to make it hard and shiny.

COOKING

FISH BALLS

Salt fish is a popular Caribbean food.

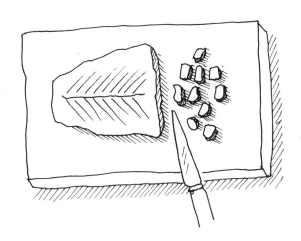

YOU WILL NEED

fish, flour, egg, milk

METHOD

1. Soak the fish well in water, then drain. Cut into small pieces.

2. Mix with flour, beaten egg and milk. Make into balls and fry until golden brown.

PINEAPPLE SHERBET

YOU WILL NEED

1 finely chopped pineapple
juice of 1 orange
568 ml (1 pt) milk
250 g (9 oz) castor sugar

METHOD

1. Mix the chopped pineapple and orange juice. Heat the milk and stir in the sugar. Leave to cool in the fridge until chilled.

2. Mix the pineapple and milk together, and stir well. Freeze until set, then decorate with pieces of pineapple.

BANANA BREAD

YOU WILL NEED

250 g (9 oz) self-raising flour
125 ml (4 1/2 fl oz) milk
125 g (4 1/2 oz) margarine
1 beaten egg
4 ripe bananas, mashed
4 drops of vanilla
pinch of nutmeg

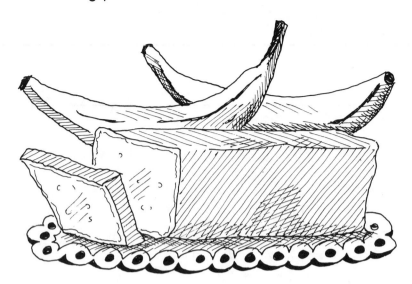

Oven temperature 190 'C/375 'F/Gas 5

METHOD

1. Blend sugar and margarine together until smooth. Add egg and bananas and beat well together.

2. Gradually mix in flour, nutmeg, salt, vanilla, and milk. Mix well together and put mixture in a baking tin. Bake for 1 hour. Cool on a baking tray. Slice and serve. Store in an airtight container.

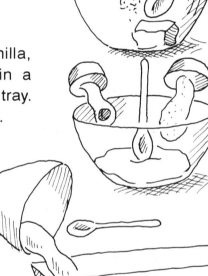

Suggested Songs: **Everybody Loves Carnival Night, Love Somebody**, from **Someone's Singing Lord**, published by A & C Black.

Little Sandy Girl, Sly Mongoose, from **Festivals (All The Year)**, by Jean Gilbert, published by Oxford University Press.

Brown Girl in the Ring, Jamaica Farewell, Mango Walk, from **Everyday Singaway-66 Songs For You To Sing**, published by Pan Books Ltd.

ST VALENTINE'S DAY

February 14th

St Valentine is the patron saint of lovers.

In Roman times, a festival of fertility rites was held in February in honour of the Goddess Februata Juno (or, according to some, the god Pan).

It is said that the Bishop Valentine, who was thrown into prison for his beliefs by the Roman Emperor Claudius II, was known as the apostle of true love. He had secretly performed marriage ceremonies for Roman soldiers who were forbidden to marry by Claudius.

Valentine fell in love with the jailer's daughter and on the day of his death, he left a note for her signed "**Your Valentine**".

In the Middle Ages, boys and girls drew slips of paper out of a hat on Valentine's Day, and accepted the one whose name was on the slip as their sweetheart, or Valentine for the year.

In Elizabethan times, Valentines were chosen by drawing lots. The gentleman then had to buy his Valentine an expensive present. This custom died out in the eighteenth century and hand-made cards replaced the presents.

Valentine's Day went out of fashion until 1926 when the cards were revived. The cards have become so popular that in 1990 more than 5 million were sent.

As well as sending cards on St Valentine's Day, young lovers also played games. They would for instance write the names of their favourite people on slips of paper, seal these in moist clay, and drop the clay balls into a bowl of water. The name on the paper slip that floated on the surface first would be their future sweetheart.

THINGS TO DO

MAKING A VALENTINE CARD

YOU WILL NEED

A4 paper, card, red shiny paper, glue, red glitter, a doily.

METHOD

1. Cut out a paper heart shape. Stick on red shiny paper, put on some glue and sprinkle with red glitter.

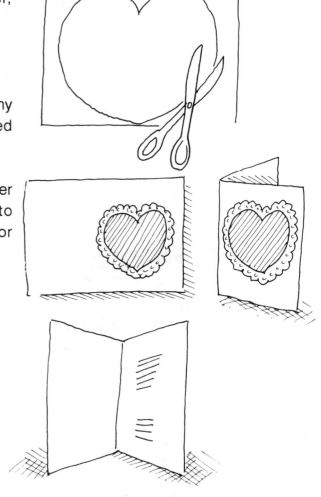

2. Stick this on the card and use strips of paper doilies to form a white border. Fold in half to form a card. Write a verse inside the card, for instance,

> 'Roses are red
> Violets are blue
> Carnations are sweet
> And so are you.
>
> And so are they
> That send you this
> And when we meet
> We'll have a kiss.'

OTHER ART IDEAS

Make a frieze with heart shapes or cut out a large heart shape and let the children sponge paint in red.

Suggested Songs: **Magic Penny, Saint Valentine's Day**, from **Alleluya-77 Songs for Thinking People**, published by A & C Black. **Valentine's Question**, from **Harlequin**, published by A & C Black. **Eve Saint Valentine's Day**, from **A Musical Calender of Festivals**, published by Ward Lock Educational. **A-tisket, A tasket**, from **Okki-Tokki-Unga**, published by A & C Black. **Do Di Li**, a Hebrew love song from, **Songs That Children Sing**, published by Oak Publications, New York.

LOVE POTIONS

Discover that by mixing colours, you can create new colours. Make a chart showing what has made one colour change to another.

<u>YOU WILL NEED</u>

Small red cabbage, water, vinegar, baking powder, 3 jars.

<u>METHOD</u>

Boil the cabbage for 10 minutes and cool. Sieve the liquid into 3 jars.

Jar 1   Add a teaspoon of vinegar, this will turn pink.

Jar 2   Add a teaspoon of baking powder, this will turn green.

Jar 3   Add a little lemon juice, this will turn pink. Change it back to purple again with baking powder.

The children can have fun experimenting with acids and alkalis. For example why not try some of these - milk, lime or lemon juice, salt, black tea, or toothpaste. Acids turn the potion pink or red. Alkalis turn the potion blue or green.

COOKING

VALENTINE TEA BISCUITS

These little biscuits can be made into heart shapes.

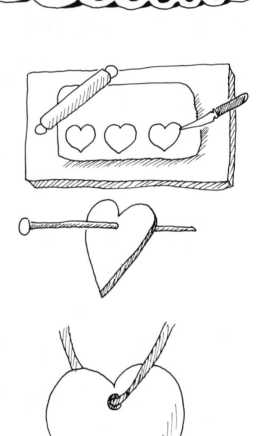

YOU WILL NEED

175 g (6 oz) margarine
225 g (8 oz) flour
175 g (6 oz) sugar
1/4 teaspoon salt
1 lemon
a pinch of bicarbonate of soda
red food colouring (optional)

Oven temperature: 180 'C/350 'F/Gas 4

METHOD

1. Cream the butter or margarine with the sugar.

2. Add the sifted flour, salt, the bicarbonate of soda, the grated rind of the lemon and one tablespoon of its juice. Add red food colouring for red biscuits.

3. Roll out thinly then cut into heart shapes. Use a skewer or a knitting needle to make a small hole at the top of the heart. Bake for 10 minutes.

4. When the biscuits have cooled, thread ribbon through the hole of each biscuit to hang around the neck of a sweetheart.

OTHER COOKING IDEAS

Make heart shaped sandwiches. Cut a cake into a heart shape and cover with pink icing sugar.

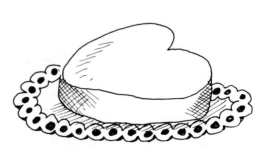

CUPID AND PSYCHE

A story to read

There was once a beautiful princess called Psyche. Her beauty made Venus, the goddess of love, very jealous. She plotted with her son Cupid to harm Psyche, and told him to pretend to fall in love with her. This way Venus thought she would be able to control Psyche. But when Cupid saw Psyche, he really did fall in love with her. But he was so afraid that his mother would find out, that he took her into the woods where she would be safe. There he visited her every night. He didn't want her to know who he really was. He was afraid if she found out that he was the son of Venus, she wouldn't love him any more. So he made her stay in the dark every time they were together.

But Psyche had a jealous sister, who made her believe that Cupid was really a horrible monster. She told her to light the lamp and see for herself. So while Cupid was fast asleep, Psyche lit a lamp. But by mistake she let a drop of hot oil from the lamp fall on his shoulder. He suddenly woke up. He was very angry with her because she hadn't done as he had asked. Cupid then ran away, never to return again.

Psyche was very sad that Cupid had gone, and she began to look for him. After many days and nights she came to a palace. But little did she know that this was the palace of Venus. The guards seized her, and took her to Venus. The goddess was very cruel to her and made her work from morning till night. Cupid, on hearing what his mother had done, rescued Psyche. And they spent the rest of their days happily together.

The name Psyche means **soul** in Greek; and this story, which is one of the later Classical myths, is usually considered to be a representation of the progression of the soul through earthly passion and the misfortune of eternal peace and joy.

The Romans pictured Cupid as a blindfolded, mischievous boy, carrying a bow and shooting at random his arrows, which caused love, hate, or disaster.

The Greeks called Cupid **Eros**, and worshipped him as the god of love and friendship. The statue of Eros can be found at Piccadily Circus in London.

PURIM

Late February/early March

THE PURIM FESTIVAL

Purim is one of the happiest of the Jewish festivals. The name Purim comes from the Hebrew word **Pur** which means dice or lots. This festival is a reminder of how the Jewish people living in Persia were saved from destruction by Esther.

THE STORY OF ESTHER

A story to read

A story is told in the Bible of how, in ancient Persia, there was a wicked man called Haman who wanted to kill all the Jews in Persia. He wanted to do this because he thought that a Jew called Mordecai had not shown him proper respect. So in order to decide on which day the Jews should die, Haman threw some dice.

But Esther, who was Mordecai's foster daughter and the King's second wife, saved the Jews by making Haman drink too much wine at a banquet.

Mordecai and Esther were so happy that they vowed that the festival of Purim should be celebrated every year.

CELEBRATING PURIM

During the Purim feast special foods are served. The turkey is sometimes chosen because it is considered to be a stupid animal - this reminds the Jews of the Persian King.

Money is given to the poor, and gifts of baked food and fruit are exchanged.

THINGS TO DO

FUN WITH FRUIT ACTIVITY

During Purim lots of fruit such as dates, grapes, figs and pomegranates are eaten.

The following activity will help to develop an understanding of the functions of the nose and tongue for smell and taste.

Cut slices from several different fruits. Blindfold a child and ask them to taste or smell the fruit and then try and identify the fruit. Note down how many they get right. Do this several times and see if the children get better at naming the fruits. Ask them which ones they found easy. This could also be done with different fruit juices.

Purim is a time for face painting, making lots of noise and having fun. Children have fancy dress parties and re-enact the story of Esther and Mordecai.

A SCROLL OF ESTHER

This is called a Megillah in Hebrew.

<u>YOU WILL NEED</u>

Kitchen roll tube, a piece of greaseproof paper cut to the width of the roll, wax crayons, clear sticky tape.

<u>METHOD</u>

Draw a picture in wax crayons on the paper, perhaps showing Esther and Mordecai celebrating victory. When the picture is finished, tape the first 2 cm (1") to the kitchen roll tube. The scroll can then be rolled round the tube.

PAPER PLATE MASKS see page 81

Play a game by putting the mask in front of the child's face, and then see if anyone recognizes them.

A GRAGGER

Purim is a happy time when people sing, dance and make a lot of noise. A gragger is a traditional noise maker. The children stamp their feet and rattle the graggers each time Haman's name is called, in order to frighten Haman away.

<u>YOU WILL NEED</u>

Small bells or rice, 15 cm (6") dowel, pipe-cleaner or wire, paper, colourful shapes, a yoghurt pot.

<u>METHOD</u>

1. Make a hole either side of the yoghurt pot and thread 5 cm (2") of wire through either hole. Then fill with rice or small bells.

2. Cover the pot with paper leaving the wire out and decorate. Place the dowel along the top of the pot and secure by twisting the wire around the dowel.

The children chant :   "Rush Rush Rush
                    Let us make a noise
                Rush Rush Rush
                    with our graggers".

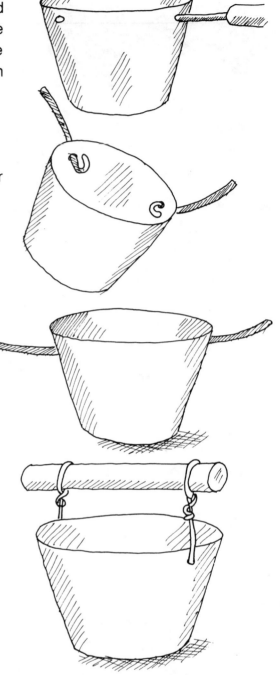

TAMBOURINES WITH PAPER PLATES

<u>YOU WILL NEED</u>

Two paper plates, paint or coloured paper, eight bottle caps, hammer and nail, wire or string.

<u>METHOD</u>

1. Decorate the paper plate either by painting or glueing colourful paper on it.

2. Make four even holes on both the plates and make a hole in each of the bottle caps with the hammer and nail.

3. Fasten two bottle caps with the wire or string through each of the holes.

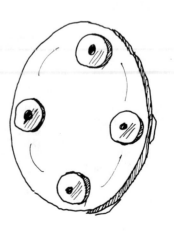

COOKING

Lots of cakes and biscuits are made during Purim. This is the time to clear the house of flour from the previous year before Passover begins.

PURIM BISCUITS (Hamantashen biscuits)

Some people cut these biscuits into shapes to look like Haman's ears. But most people make them into triangles from a round shape. This represents the three cornered hat that Haman wore.

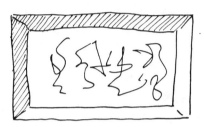

YOU WILL NEED

75 g (3 oz) plain flour
50 g (2 oz) butter, softened
50 g (2 oz) sugar
25 g (1 oz) ground almonds or hazel nuts
1/2 teaspoon cinnamon

Oven temperature: 180 'C/350 'F/ Gas 4

METHOD

1. Lightly flour a baking tray. Beat the butter and sugar together in a bowl. Gradually add the flour a little at a time and knead well together. Knead in the nuts. When the dough feels smooth, cut into rounds then fold and pinch three sides of the dough to form the hat.

2. Place well apart on the tray. Sprinkle the centre of each biscuit with a little cinnamon. Bake for 15-20 minutes. Remove from the oven and cool on a wire rack.

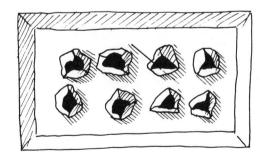

POPPY SEED BISCUITS

For these biscuits, it is best to leave the biscuit dough overnight before dividing into shapes.

YOU WILL NEED

225 g (8 oz) unsalted butter   175 g (6 oz) sugar
275 g (10 oz) flour   75 g (3 oz) poppy seed
1 teaspoon vanilla essence   pinch salt
1 1/2 teaspoon baking powder

Oven temperature: 190'C/375'F/ Gas 5.

METHOD

Cream butter and sugar. Add the eggs, poppy seed, vanilla, and mix well. Add the flour, salt and baking powder. The dough will be a little sticky. Leave in the fridge overnight. Next day, make into 5 cm (2") circles and bake on a greased baking sheet for 10-12 minutes.

CHICK-PEAS WITH TOMATOES

Chick-peas are a traditional Purim food. (Esther did not eat the rich food served at the Persian court). To be sure of keeping the Jewish food laws, Esther ate only fruit and vegetables. The chick-peas served at the Purim feast are in remembrance of Esther's respect for the Jewish laws.

YOU WILL NEED

400 g (14 oz) can chick-peas
1 tablespoon tomato purée   4 tomatoes
1 small onion, sliced   salt and pepper

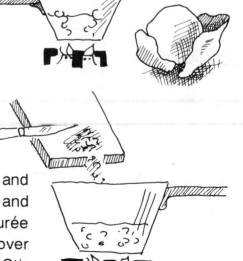

METHOD

1. Drop the tomatoes into a pan of boiling water and quickly remove. Peel and chop the tomatoes and place in a pan with the sliced onion, tomato purée and seasoning. Bring the mixture to the boil. Cover with a lid and simmer for 30 minutes. Stir occasionally. Add the chick-peas and serve either hot or cold.

SONGS SUNG AT PURIM

To the tune of SING A SONG OF SIXPENCE

Sing a song of Purim
What a happy time.
Boys and girls enjoy it,
Purim cakes and wine.
We sing of good Queen Esther,
And of Mordechai the Jew.
Of King Asasuarus,
And wicked Haman too.

To the tune of FRÈRE JAQUES

Today it's Purim,
Today it's Purim.
A lovely day,
A lovely day.
We will have a party,
We will have a party.
Hip Hoorah, Hip Hoorah.

To the tune of TWINKLE TWINKLE

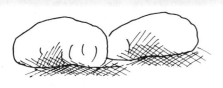

Hamantashen we will eat, Hamantashen are
so sweet.
One for you and one for me,
Now let's eat them, one two three.
Hamantashen we will eat,
Hamantashen are so sweet.

To the tune of PAT-A-CAKE

Pat-a-cake, pat-a-cake baker's man,
Make me a Hamantashen, fast as you can.
Roll it and fold it and make corners three,
Make one for Mummy and Daddy and me.

ANI PURIM a poem for Purim

I am Purim
I am Purim
I make a funny show
I do appear just once a year
And then away I go.

ST DAVID'S DAY

March 1st

St David is the patron saint of Wales. Daffodils and leeks are the national symbols of Wales and are worn by the Welsh on St David's Day.

THE DAFFODIL

I wander'd lonely as a cloud,
That floats on high o'er vales and hills.
When all at once I saw a crowd,
A host, of golden daffodils;
Beside the lake, beneath the trees,
Fluttering and dancing in the breeze.

By William Wordsworth

THINGS TO DO

MAKE A DAFFODIL

<u>YOU WILL NEED</u>

Paper, paint, paper straw, an egg box.

<u>METHOD</u>

1. Cut out the shape of a daffodil in paper and staple it onto the straw.

2. Cut out one section of the egg box and then cut out small triangles along the top to form zig-zags. Glue the bottom of the egg box to the centre of the flower and paint it yellow. Paint the stem green and when it is dry staple it to the daffodil.

THE STORY OF ST DAVID

A story to read

St David was a very important church man who lived in South Wales. He lived a simple life as a Christian and worked very hard in many churches all over Wales. There are 53 churches named after him.

St David was a very kind man and he helped many people get better when they were ill. He even helped the blind to see, and the lame to walk.

St David could make water appear from nowhere. One day he discovered there was no fresh water, and the people in the town were very thirsty. So St David prayed for water and do you know what happened? A well sprang up at his feet. He did this in other part of Wales as well and each time a well would spring up.

After all his hard work, St David was made the Archbishop of Wales.

DAFFODIL SUNDAY

In England the first Sunday in April is called Daffodil Sunday. In Victorian times, families would walk out together to pick daffodils from their gardens and take them to local hospitals to give to the sick. In some parts of Britain the first daffodil is thought to bring luck, but misfortune is said to await those who pluck a single bloom and bring it into the house.

If you buy daffodils they should not be mixed with other flowers as the stems excrete a poisonous juice.

HINA-MATSURI A Japanese Doll Festival

March 3rd

This is the day when Japanese girls display their collection of ceremonial dolls, which have been passed from mother to daughter. The making of these dolls is a very old art. The earlier figures were warriors, which were placed at the graves of nobles, in place of human sacrifice. Very simple dolls of paper or bamboo are believed to have magic powers. It is believed that dolls can take away evil or illness, guard little babies, and they can bring fair weather.

At least fifteen dolls are arranged in front of a screen. They are placed in special order, with the Emperor and Empress on the highest shelf. When the festival is over, the dolls are carefully packed away, until the next year.

This is a time when the girls visit each other's houses, to admire the dolls and exchange sweet cakes and rice wine.

This is also the month of cherry blossoms, or **Sakura**, the national flower of Japan. Parties known as **Hanami** (flower viewing) are held in the open air under the blossom and so the lovely decorations for this festival are cherry blossoms.

Today, this day is known as Children's Day.

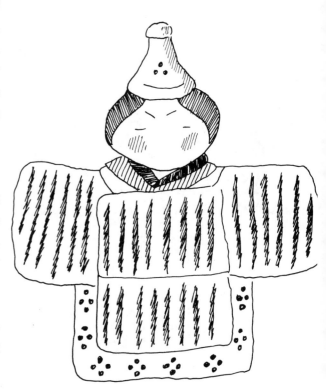

THINGS TO DO

MAKE A HINA-MATSURI DOLL

On Dolls Day the children can either bring in their own dolls to display or have fun making their own.

<u>YOU WILL NEED</u>

Baker's clay (see page 103), string.

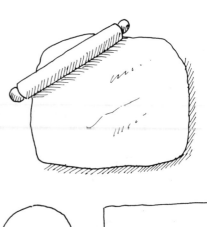

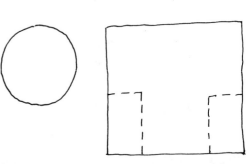

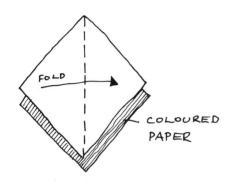

FOLD

COLOURED PAPER

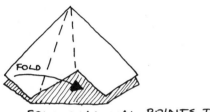

FOLD

FOLD DIAGONAL POINTS TO LIE ON DIAGONAL

FOLD LEFT HAND LAYERS ON SLANT

FOLD BOTTOM FOR BASE

CUT OUT FACE AND GLUE ON NECK

METHOD

Roll out the baker's clay and cut out a circle and a square. These will form the doll as shown. Make a small hole at the top of the circle. Once the doll has cooked, thread the string through the hole. These can either be worn or hung up.

HOW TO MAKE AN ORIGAMI DOLL

It is traditional at the end of the festival for the children to make dolls of paper and cloth. The dolls are then placed in a straw basket and set afloat on the rivers, to be swept away to another world.

COOKING

TRADITIONAL FOOD

Rice-cake is made from rice which is pounded. Three layers are formed, the top is green, the middle is white and the bottom layer is pink. This is then cut into a diamond shape.

Why not make an ordinary cake cut into a doll shape using this idea?

Sakura-Mochi is always eaten at Hina-Matsuri. These are small pink rice-cakes wrapped in a cherry leaf pickled in brine.

GIRLS DAY by Mayuko Kawaguchi, 10 yrs old

On 3rd March, we have Girls Day. We decorate Japanese dolls wearing kimonos. We eat rice-cake cubes, long shaped rice-cakes and drink a sweet dry sake. This sake is like a sweet juice, so children can drink it. When I drink a sweet sake, I feel good and a little bit hot, so I like to drink it. There are a King, a Queen, three maids and five musical band dolls. They are wearing old-fashioned kimonos. I like kimonos and dolls, so I like Girls Day very much. We do Girls Day in order to drive away the evils in our hearts.

Suggested Songs: **Sakura**, from **Songs that Children Sing**, published by Oak Publications, New York.

ST PATRICK'S DAY

March 17th

St Patrick is the patron saint of Ireland. He came from a noble Scottish family.

A story to read

At the age of sixteen St Patrick was captured by pirates, and taken to Ireland. Here he was then sold as a slave to some pig farmers. He worked for seven whole years, until one day some sailors helped him to escape.

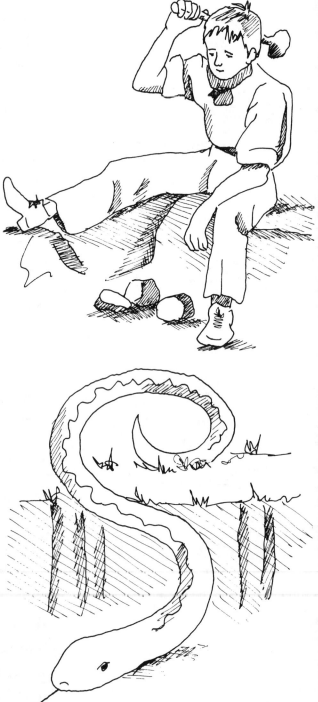

He then travelled far and wide until he reached a place called Italy. It was here that he decided that he would work for the church. After many years of study he was made a bishop and was told to go back to Ireland and teach the word of God.

When he returned he found out that the King of Tara had ruled that every fire in Ireland must be put out at Easter time and only re-lighted from a fire at his castle on the Hill of Tara.

St Patrick disobeyed this rule and was caught lighting his own fire. He was then taken to the King, who was very angry with him. But St Patrick explained to the King that he had made the fire because he wanted to remember Jesus Christ who had risen from the dead on Easter morning. And to St Patrick's surprise, the King forgave him.

St Patrick was also a very brave man. You see there used to be many snakes in Ireland, and the people were very frightened of them. So one day St Patrick made all the snakes follow him up to the top of a high cliff. On reaching the top all the snakes fell off the cliff and into the sea. Since then, no snakes have been seen in Ireland.

THINGS TO DO

THE SHAMROCK

The shamrock, a small clover-like plant, which bears three leaves on each stem, is said to have been used by St Patrick as an illustration of the Trinity.

So, in honour of the saint, if you live where shamrocks grow, you must wear one in your hat on March 17th. In America people wear little artificial shamrocks. It is the custom to wear something green, and to have corned beef and cabbage dinner.

MIXING GREEN FOR THE SHAMROCK

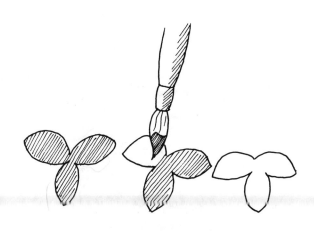

<u>YOU WILL NEED</u>

Green, white, and black paint, 6-8 shamrock shapes cut from paper.

<u>METHOD</u>

1. Mix a very light green and paint the first shamrock. Now add a little black paint and paint the next one.

2. Continue until the green is very dark. By using white paint you can reverse this process. Once the shamrocks are dry, ask the children to place them on the table in order of colour, from light to dark.

POTATO PRINT SNAKES

<u>YOU WILL NEED</u>

Potato, paint, large sheet of paper.

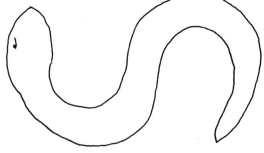

<u>METHOD</u>

Cut out a snake shape from the paper. Cut the potato in half and score out a shamrock on one half and wiggly snake lines on the other. Give the potato a handle by cutting out two pieces from either side at the top of the potato. Print shapes on the paper snake using the potatoes dipped in paint.

SNAKE FROM A PLATE

<u>YOU WILL NEED</u>

White paper plate, crayons, coloured shapes, cotton thread.

<u>METHOD</u>

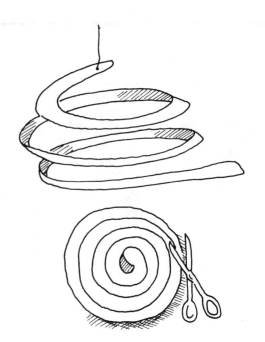

1. Starting from the middle of the plate draw the head of the snake, and then continue with a spiral 15 mm wide all the way round the plate.

2. Colour the plate and decorate with coloured shapes. Then cut along the spiral all the way round. Thread the head of the snake with some cotton and hang from the wall or ceiling.

SPROUTING A POTATO

Potatoes at one time formed a very important part in the diet of the Irish people, and they were introduced into Ireland first in 1587. In 1846 a terrible plague hit the potato crop and half a million peasants are said to have died from starvation. At this time three million Irish people emigrated to America. Queen Victoria even asked that prayers should be offered up for the potato in every church, chapel and synagogue.

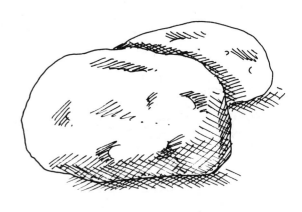

<u>YOU WILL NEED</u>

A potato that has started to sprout, a shoe box.

<u>METHOD</u>

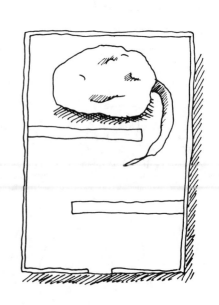

1. Put the potato in one end of the shoe box and cut a half inch hole at the other end of the box. Place two pieces of cardboard either side of the box a short distance away from each other, to form a maze.

2. Place the lid on the box. Put the box on a window sill with the hole facing the light. The shoots will eventually find their way out into the light. Every few days check the progress of the roots.

SHAMROCKS AND SNAKES

From Baker's Clay

<u>YOU WILL NEED</u>

4 cups flour
1 cup of salt
1 1/2 cups of water

Oven temperature: 180 C/350 F/Gas 4

<u>METHOD</u>

1. Mix all the ingredients together. Knead until firm as you would with dough.

2. Roll the baker's clay and cut out shamrock leaves and a stem.

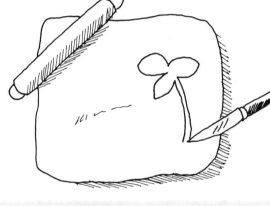

3. Roll the clay into snake shapes.

4. Carefully place the completed dough on a baking tray. Bake in the oven for about 45 minutes, until lightly brown, and firm to touch.

5. Once the clay has cooled the children can paint it. For a harder finish coat with varnish.

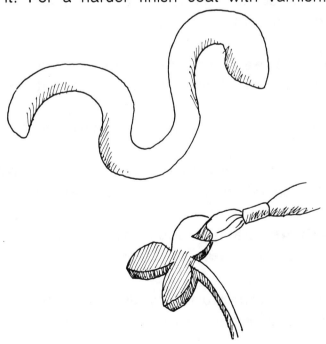

Suggested Song: **St Patrick Was a Gentleman**, from **A Musical Calender of Festivals**, published by Ward Lock Educational.

BOOKS ON ART

Arts and Crafts Around the Jewish Calender, by Shoshana Mermeistein and Chava Shapiro, published by Torah Umesorah Publications, 229 Park Avenue South, New York 10003.

Bright Ideas, Seasonal Activities, published by Scholastic Publications Ltd, Marlborough House, Holly Walk, Leamington Spa, Warwickshire CV32 4LS.

BOOKS FOR EASTER

Pancakes and Painted Eggs, by Jean Chapman, published by Hodder and Stoughton.

The Easter Book, by Jenny Vaughan, published by Macdonald Educational.

The Easter Book, by Felicity Trotman, published by Hippo Books Scholastic Publications Ltd.

Easter Book, by Julian Fox, published by Wayland.

BOOKS ON FESTIVALS

A Calender of Feasts, Cattern Cakes, and Lace, by Julia Jones and Barbara Deer, published by Dorling Kindersley Ltd.

Bright Ideas, Festivals, by Jill Bennett and Archie Miller, published by Scholastic Publications Ltd.

Carnival, by Jon Mayled, published by Wayland.

Children's Festivals from Many Lands, by Nina Millen, published by Friendship Press N.Y.

Festivals, Family and Food, by Diana & Judy Large, published by Hawthorn Press.

Festive Occasions, by Judy Ridgeway, published by Oxford University Press.

Festivals (all the year), by Jean Gilbert, published by Oxford University Press.

Festivals, By Olivia Bennett, published by Bell & Hyman Publishing.

Festivals, Ramadan and Eid Ul-Fitr, by Rosalind Kerven, published by Macmillan Education.

Hindu Festivals, by Swasti Mitter, published by Wayland.

Hindi Nursery Rhymes, by Sarita Sethi Hema Piwan, Mantra Publishing, 5 Alexandra Grove, London N12 8NU.

Jewish Festivals, by Reuben Turner, published by Wayland.

Crafts in Action Throughout the Jewish Year, by Judith Rabin, published by J.N.F Company.

Muslim Festivals, by M.M Ahsan, published by Wayland.

Sikh Festivals, by Dr. Sukhbir Singh Kapoor, published by Wayland.

BOOKS ON FOOD

Exploring Caribbean Food in Britain, by Floella Benjamin, published by Mantra Publishing.

Food Around the World, by Jenny & Judy Ridgeway, published by Oxford University Press.

Japanese Food and Drink, by Lesley Downer, published by Wayland.

Jewish Holiday Kitchen, by Joan Nathan, published by Schoken Books N.Y.

BOOKS FOR SPRING

The Seasons Spring, by David Lambert, published by Wayland.

The Springtime Book, by James Reeves, published by William Heinemann.

A Book of Spring, by Colin and Moira Maclean, published by Studio Vista/Cassell.

BOOKS ON NATURE

A Country Book, by Diane Elson, published by World's Works Ltd.

Discover Nature, by Midas Dekker, published by Exley Publishers.

Nature Through the Seasons, by Peter Gerrard, published by Midas Books.

The Book of the Year, by Jane Burton, published by Frederick Warne.

Your Book of the Year, by Muriel Goaman, published by Faber and Faber.

BOOKS ON SCIENCE

Usborne Science and Experiments Ecology, published by Usborne.

The Usborne Book of Simple Science, by Angela Wilkes & David Mostyn, published by Usborne.

First Book of Science, by Gaby Waters, published by Usborne.

Science is Fun, Floating and Sinking, by Ed Catherall, published by Wayland.

Exciting Things to do with Nature, published by Marshall Cavendish Books Ltd.